PIANO CHORD VOICINGS
in all styles

by Mark Harrison

PLAYBACK+
Speed • Pitch • Balance • Loop

To access audio, visit:
www.halleonard.com/mylibrary

Enter Code
6825-8522-9538-4666

ISBN 978-1-70513-674-4

Visit Hal Leonard Online at
www.halleonard.com

World headquarters, contact:
Hal Leonard
7777 West Bluemound Road
Milwaukee, WI 53213
Email: info@halleonard.com

In Europe, contact:
Hal Leonard Europe Limited
1 Red Place
London, W1K 6PL
Email: info@halleonardeurope.com

In Australia, contact:
Hal Leonard Australia Pty. Ltd.
4 Lentara Court
Cheltenham, Victoria, 3192 Australia
Email: info@halleonard.com.au

T0086987

CONTENTS

INTRODUCTION

Welcome to *Piano Chord Voicings in All Styles*. The goal of this book is to provide you with chord voicing examples for a wide range of classic and modern popular styles.

Some of you may be wondering, "What is a chord voicing?" Well, we use this term to describe a specific interpretation of a given chord symbol, for example in a chart or fake book. "Voicing" the chords appropriately for the musical style you are playing is a vital part of making your performance sound more professional.

A chord voicing may be different from the literal spelling of a chord, in one (or more) of the following ways: adding extensions or alterations to the chord, subtracting notes from the chord, doubling notes of the chord in either or both hands, redistributing the notes of the chord between the hands, using various shapes (specific interval combinations) in either or both hands, and so on.

For each of the 18 styles featured in this book, we'll show you sample voicings that are idiomatic for the style, followed by rhythmic style examples showing how these voicings are typically used (with play-along tracks).

This book introduces a lot of keyboard harmony and voicing concepts. If you would like more in-depth information on any of the topics mentioned, please check out the Further Reading section at the end.

Good luck with your Chord Voicings on the piano!

– Mark Harrison

About the Audio

On the accompanying audio tracks, you'll find recordings of all the music examples in the book. The voicing examples are all recorded as solo keyboard tracks, with the left-hand part on the left channel and the right-hand part on the right channel. The rhythmic style examples are all recorded as full-band tracks, with the rhythm section on the left channel and the piano part on the right channel. To play along with the band on these tracks, simply turn down the right channel. You can gain full access to the audio by visiting www.halleonard.com/mylibrary and inputting the unique code printed on the first page of this book.

About the Author

Mark Harrison is a professional keyboardist, composer/arranger, and music educator/author based in Los Angeles. He has recorded three albums as a contemporary jazz bandleader (with the Mark Harrison Quintet), and performs regularly throughout Southern California with the Steely Dan tribute band Doctor Wu. Mark's TV music credits include *Saturday Night Live, American Justice, Celebrity Profiles, America's Most Wanted, True Hollywood Stories,* and many others. Mark is an endorsed artist/educator for Dexibell keyboards, performing at the world-renowned NAMM music industry trade show in Los Angeles.

Mark has held faculty positions at the Grove School of Music and at the University of Southern California (Thornton School of Music). He runs a busy online teaching studio, catering to the needs of professional and aspiring musicians worldwide. Mark's students include Grammy® winners, hit songwriters, members of the Boston Pops and Los Angeles Philharmonic orchestras, and first-call touring musicians with major acts. He has written over 30 music instruction books, as well as various Master Class articles for *Keyboard* magazine and other publications.

For further information on Mark's educational products and online lessons, please visit www.harrisonmusic.com.

CHAPTER 1

BLUES

Blues is an indigenous American music style that emerged in the late 19th century, flourished and developed in the 20th century, and laid the foundations for modern-day R&B and rock styles. Blues has also been closely intertwined with jazz since its inception, and is a major influence on all classic and contemporary jazz styles.

Our first voicing example uses 3rds and 7ths of various dominant 7th chords in the right hand, over the chord roots in the left hand.

Blues Voicing Example #1

🔊 Track 1

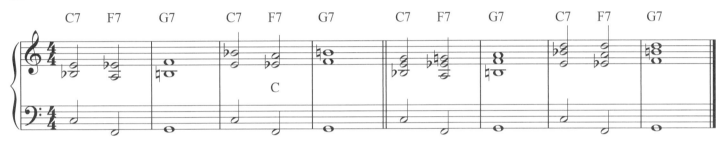

All these chord symbols are for **dominant 7th** chords. The dominant chord is the basis of most blues harmony and progressions.

A dominant 7th is a four-note consisting of major 3rd, perfect 5th, and minor 7th intervals above the root—so the first C7 chord symbol shown above would be literally spelled as C, E, G, and B♭. In the first voicing shown above for the C7 chord though, we are using only the 3rd and 7th (E and B♭) in the right hand, placed above the root of C in the left hand. This type of skeletal **seven-three** (or three-seven) voicing is a staple of blues and jazz styles. All the dominant chords in the first four measures are voiced in this way.

Then in the next four measures, an extra note has been added above the seven-three voicing in the right hand. This extra note is either:

- the **5th** of the chord (on the C7 in measure 5, and G7 in measure 8)
- the **9th** of the chord (on the F7 in measure 5, G7 in measure 6, and C7 in measure 7)
- the **13th** of the chord (on the F7 in measure 7)

I refer to this type of voicing as **seven-three extended** in my books and classes.

Blues and jazz musicians will routinely add these unaltered upper extensions (i.e., 9ths and 13ths) to dominant chords, even though the chord symbols will often just be basic four-part (7th) chord symbols as shown above.

Our first style example uses the basic seven-three voicings from the first four measures in Track 1, over a 12-bar blues progression in C:

Blues Style Example #1

 Track 2

This is in a jazz-blues swing style, with the right hand playing rhythmically syncopated seven-three voicings, and the left hand playing a root-and-5th pattern on each chord.

Note the **Swing 8ths** text shown above the music: instead of the eighth notes dividing the beat exactly in half, the beat is instead divided in a two-thirds/one-third ratio. This is equivalent to playing each pair of eighth notes as a quarter note/eighth-note triplet, and is common in classic blues and jazz styles. Check out the audio track to get comfortable with this important "swing" feel.

The next style example uses the seven-three extended voicings from the last four measures in Track 1, over the same 12-bar blues progression in C:

Blues Style Example #2

 Track 3

This is similar to the previous example in Track 2, except the right hand is now adding some 5ths, 9ths, and 13ths above the seven-three voicings on these dominant chords. These three-note right-hand voicings create a more sophisticated sound.

Our next voicing example uses four-part **block voicings** in the right hand, for the same C7, F7, and G7 dominant chords.

Blues Voicing Example #2

Track 4

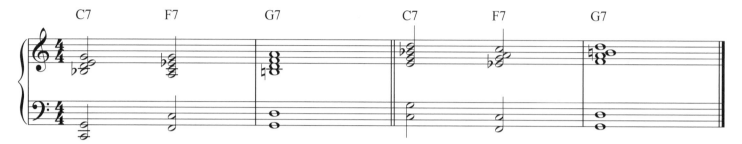

We use the term block voicing to describe the use of four different pitches within a one-octave range, which produces a dense and saturated sound. By this definition, the literal spellings of all common four-part chords would qualify as block voicings.

Earlier in this chapter, we reviewed the literal spelling of the C7 (dominant 7th) chord: C, E, G, and B♭. This isn't quite what we see, though, in the right hand at the start of the first measure above: we do have the E, G, and B♭, but instead of the C we have the D.

This is equivalent to the 3rd, 5th, 7th, and 9th of the dominant chord; in other words, we have upgraded the dominant 7th chord to a **dominant 9th**. Again, this is often done in response to the basic (four-part) dominant 7th chord symbols shown above.

Another way to think of this right-hand voicing (which I recommend) is to realize we have built a **minor 7th (♭5th) chord** from the 3rd of the dominant chord. In the first measure above, the first right-hand voicing is actually a 2nd-inversion Em7(♭5) chord; this is built from the 3rd (E) of the overall C7 chord, technically upgrading it to a C9.

Similarly, we have built an Am7(♭5) from the 3rd of the F7 chord, and a Bm7(♭5) from the 3rd of the G7 chord. In measures 3-4 we're using the same upper-structure minor 7th (♭5) chords over the C7, F7 and G7, but in different inversions.

In the left hand we are playing the root and 5th of each chord, which gives solid support to the right-hand voicings, and is suitable for more contemporary blues and blues-rock settings.

Our next style example uses these upper-structure block voicings from Track 4, this time in a blues-rock shuffle style.

Blues Style Example #3

 Track 5

This follows a 12-bar format similar to the earlier blues examples. Note the syncopated accents used by the right-hand block voicings, over the driving root-5th and root-6th interval pattern in the left hand. This is a typical blues shuffle feel; again, watch out for the Swing 8ths direction as discussed earlier.

CHAPTER 2

CALM PIANO

Calm Piano is a peaceful, relaxing style that has its origins in the 1980s New Age genre. The calming, meditative effect typically is created with **arpeggios** (playing notes of the chord one-at-a-time, or broken-chord style) within basic harmonies.

Our first voicing example shows some left-hand diatonic triads in the key of F, with inversions to stay just below the middle C area. As chord arpeggios are so central to this style, each triad voicing is followed by a corresponding eighth-note arpeggio pattern:

Calm Piano Voicing Example #1

Track 6

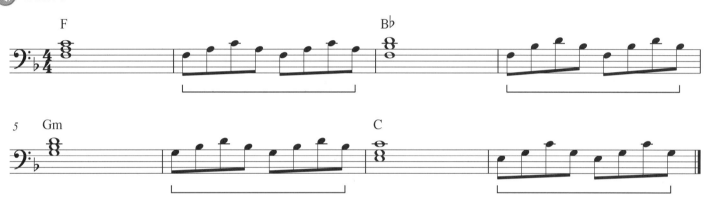

Each pair of measures in this example consists of a whole-note triad followed by a basic eighth-note arpeggio pattern for the same chord. Note the pedal markings used: in Calm Piano styles, and piano ballad styles in general, you'll normally need to depress the sustain pedal for the duration of each chord.

Our first style example uses the left-hand arpeggios shown above to support a simple right-hand melody typical for the style.

Calm Piano Style Example #1

Track 7

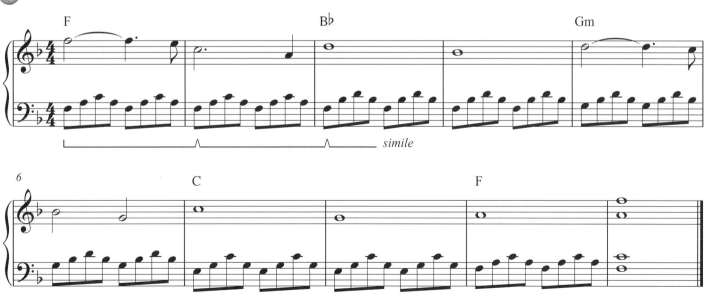

A smooth, flowing effect is created with the left-hand arpeggios; the underlying triads use **voice leading** to move closely between inversions, avoiding large interval skips. Again, remember to use the sustain pedal during each chord, releasing at the point of chord change.

Triad harmony, rather than using larger chords, is common in this style, because it results in the least tension and dissonance.

Our next voicing example focuses on left-hand voicings, this time using **open** triads for a different texture. We use the term open to describe a triad that extends over a range greater than an octave, as a result of moving the **middle note up one octave**. For example, the first measure in Track 8 contains the notes D-A-F from bottom to top; this is the result of moving the 3rd of the D minor triad (F) up one octave. Each open triad voicing is followed by two arpeggio patterns: the first uses eighth-note rhythms, and the second uses 16th-note rhythms.

Calm Piano Voicing Example #2

 Track 8

By the way, don't worry if your left hand can't stretch the larger intervals needed for the open triads in measures 1 and 6 above. Those voicings are there to show you where the arpeggio patterns are derived from.

When playing the left-hand arpeggios, I recommend you skip over the notes without stretching too much. Let the sustain pedal do the work!

Note that in the 16th-note arpeggio patterns above (measures 4-5 and 9-10) we're also adding the **9th** to each chord. The 9th is the most common chord extension to add, in Calm Piano styles.

Our next style example uses the eighth-note left-hand arpeggios from Track 8 (measures 2-3 and 7-8), below a right-hand part supported mostly with 6th intervals, with some 4ths and 5ths.

Calm Piano Style Example #2

🔊 Track 9

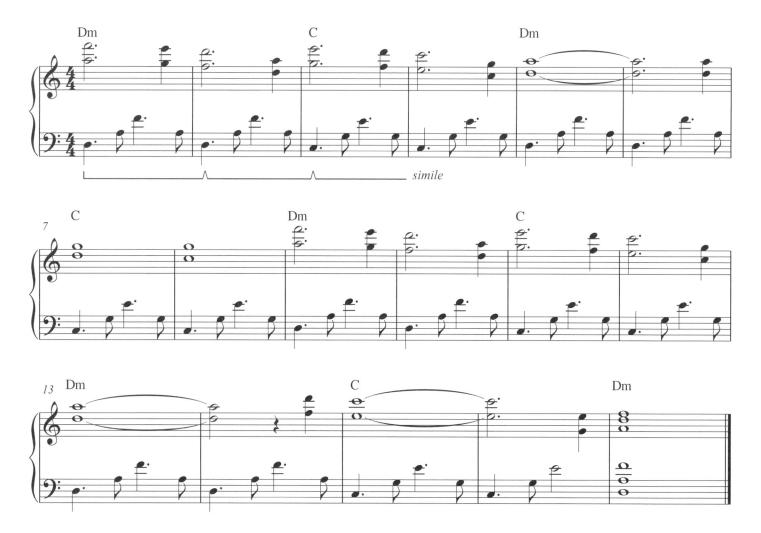

For the most part, the right hand employs a "6th interval below melody" technique, imparting a warm, consonant sound well-suited to Calm Piano, and piano ballad styles in general. However, in some places the 6th intervals have been reduced to 4ths or 5ths. This is either to conform to the triad harmony or to add an extension such as the 9th, which is typical for the style.

Our last style example uses the 16th-note left-hand arpeggios from Track 8 (measures 4-5 and 9-10), below a sparse right-hand melody.

Calm Piano Style Example #3

🔊 Track 10

Here, the right-hand melody is a single-note part, predominantly active during beat 4 of each measure, where the left-hand arpeggios are not subdividing. All this results in a "to-and-fro," a rhythmic conversation between hands that is normal for this style.

CHAPTER 3

CLASSIC ROCK

Classic Rock is a genre associated with the iconic rock artists of the 1970s and '80s. The style predominantly uses triad voicings, most often with eighth-note rhythmic subdivisions.

Our first example shows a mix of major triad and root-5th **power-chord** voicings. The chord progression uses a series of circle-of-4ths chord movements (C to G to D), common in Classic Rock.

> **Theory note:** We define **circle-of-4ths** as a series of **four-to-one** relationships; i.e., C is a IV of G, G is a IV of D, and so on. This is a more contemporary view of the circle-of-4ths, which you may not have encountered. There's much more about this in our other books. (See Further Reading section on page 82.)

Classic Rock Voicing Example #1

 Track 11

In measures 1–4, we see major triads in the right hand over root notes in the left hand. Note the use of triad inversions to voice lead smoothly between chords.

Then in measures 5–8, we see root-5th voicings in the right hand (with either the root or 5th doubled, one octave apart) over root-5th voicings in the left hand. These are often referred to as power-chord voicings, as they mimic the typical overdriven guitar voicings in rock styles; when the guitar sound is distorted or overloaded, anything other than the root and 5th of the chord is muddy and unusable.

Our first style example uses the triad voicings from Track 11 (measures 1–4), in a rock shuffle style.

Classic Rock Style Example #1
🔊 Track 12

Here, the left hand is strengthening the roots of each chord with octaves, providing a solid eighth-note rhythmic foundation. For the correct shuffle feel, be sure to observe the Swing 8ths direction. The right-hand triads are using various syncopated eighth-note rhythms and anticipations, landing ahead of the beat, all of which is typical for the style.

In measures 6 and 8, the C and D major chords are embellished with fills from the C and D pentatonic scales, respectively.

Our next style example combines the different voicings from Track 11: the right-hand major triads (with left-hand roots) from measures 1-4, and the right-hand power-chord root-5th voicings (with left-hand root-5th intervals) from measures 5-8.

Classic Rock Style Example #2

Track 13

Our next voicing example uses various upper-structure triads in the right hand, placed over chord roots in the left hand. These upper-structure triads are grouped in pairs; i.e., we are moving from triad to another, over the same root note. In my books and classes, I use the term **alternating triads** to describe this type of voicing approach. This is a common sound in Classic Pop and Rock styles, especially.

Classic Rock Voicing Example #2

Track 14

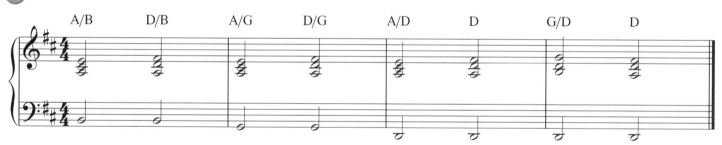

Let's take a closer look at the first measure above, to make sure we understand this concept. Here we're alternating between an A major triad and D major triad, using inversions to voice lead, over the root note of B. This is often heard and used in the context of a big-tent **Bmi7 chord**—in other words, moving between these two upper triads provides interior motion and upper extensions with respect to a Bmi7 chord.

If we now look at the two individual voicings in the first measure:

- The A major triad is built from the 7th of the overall Bmi7 chord. This adds the 9th (C♯) and 11th (E) to the Bmi7. These are normally safe and stable upper extensions to add on minor chords.

- The D major triad is built from the 3rd of the overall Bmi7 chord. This just contains the basic chord tones (3rd, 5th, and 7th) of the overall chord.

So when we move from the A/B voicing to the D/B voicing, we're essentially moving between two versions of a Bmi7 chord: the first with upper extensions (i.e., 9th and 11th), and the second with more basic chord tones. As such, this imparts a type of resolving interior motion, within the overall chord. In my other books, I refer to this particular alternating triad pair as ♭**7 to ♭3 triads on a minor chord**, as these triads are built from the 7th and 3rd of the minor chord, respectively.

Similarly, in the next two measures:

- In measure 2, the same A and D major triads are heard in the context of a big-tent G major chord, as G is now in the bass. These upper-structure triads add various tones/extensions to the overall G major chord (i.e., the 7th, 9th, ♯11th, and 13th). I refer to this alternating triad pair as **9 to 5 triads on a major chord** in my other books.

- In measure 3, the same A and D major triads are heard in the context of a big-tent D major chord, as D is now in the bass. The A major triad adds the 7th and 9th to the overall D major chord. I refer to this alternating triad pair as **5 to 1 triads on a major chord** in my other books.

In measure 4, there is a different principle at work: although moving between the G/D and D voicings will often be used to give motion within an overall D major chord, the G major triad adds no useful upper extensions to the overall D major chord; rather, the G major triad is heard as a passing chord that resolves into the D major triad. I refer to this alternating triad pair as **4 to 1 triads on a major chord** in my other books.

Note that each upper-structure triad voicing in Track 14 has its own chord symbol (i.e., A/B, D/B, and so on). However, you may instead see more collective (aggregate) chord symbols used instead; i.e., **Bm** or **Bm7** for the whole first measure, per the explanation above. For the following style example, I've written the chord symbols in this manner, so you see the different ways this type of harmony can be notated.

So, on to our last style example, which uses all the right-hand alternating-triad voicings from Track 14, together with a typical driving pop/rock rhythm pattern in the left hand.

Classic Rock Style Example #3

 Track 15

The right-hand triads use various anticipations (landing ahead of the beat), which, together with the steady driving left-hand pattern, is typical in Classic Pop/Rock.

Again, note the collective chord symbols used here: in the first measure we are moving between D and A major triads in the right hand (similar to the first measure in Track 14), which over B in the bass creates a **Bm** (or Bm7) harmonic impression.

CHAPTER 4

CLASSIC R&B

These days, R&B is a catch-all category, incorporating various musical sub-styles such as soul, funk, hip-hop, dance-pop, and so on. The term Classic R&B is commonly associated with the soulful pop/funk and ballad recordings from the 1970s and '80s. These styles often use larger chords, compared to basic pop and rock, and more 16th-note rhythms.

Our first voicing example uses upper-structure triads in the right hand, placed over left-hand root-7th intervals in measures 1-3, and a root-5th interval in measure 4. Left-hand root-7th intervals are a staple of jazz piano, and also work well for more sophisticated R&B/pop styles.

Classic R&B Voicing Example #1

Track 16

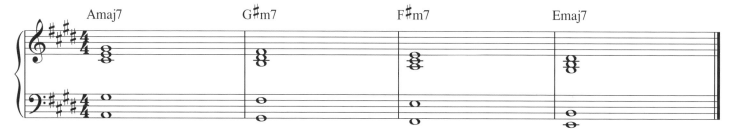

Let's take a look at the upper-structure triad voicings used here:
- In measure 1, the right-hand C# minor triad is built from the 3rd of the overall Amaj7 chord.
- In measure 2, the right-hand B major triad is built from the 3rd of the overall G#m7 chord.
- In measure 3, the right-hand A major triad is built from the 3rd of the overall F#m7 chord.
- In measure 4, the right-hand G# minor triad is built from the 3rd of the overall Emaj7 chord.

The left-hand root-7th voicings will sound muddy if played too low: the F#-E interval in measure 3 is near the bottom of the useful range for pop styles. We switched to the root-5th interval in measure 4 to avoid playing the root-7th voicing too low on the Emaj7 chord.

Note that these voicings add no extra chord tones/extensions with respect to the four-part chord symbols used; by building the right-hand upper triads from the 3rd in each measure, we are essentially splitting each chord by placing the 3rd, 5th, and 7th in the right hand (over the root-7th or root-5th in the left hand). This gives us a professional-sounding result that is authentic for the style.

Our first style example uses the upper-structure triad voicings from Track 16, in an R&B ballad style.

Classic R&B Style Example #1

Track 17

In each measure, the right-hand upper triads are played with characteristic 16th-note rhythms, landing on the last 16th of beat 1, just ahead of beat 2. In measures 5-8 within beat 4, the right hand lands on the second 16th, further adding to the syncopated effect.

The left hand holds the root of each chord on the bottom (with the pinky) while reinforcing the right-hand rhythms with either the 7th or 5th of each chord. All of this creates a recognizable R&B ballad-style effect.

Our next voicing example uses various upper-structure block (four-part) chords in the right hand, placed over a mix of octave, root-7th, and root-5th voicings in the left hand. We saw a similar example of upper-structure block voicings earlier, in Track 4, for dominant chords. Here, however, we've created voicings for a mix of major, minor, and **suspended** dominant chords, all of which are typically used in R&B/pop styles.

Classic R&B Voicing Example #2

Track 18

Note that the upper-structure block shapes use inversions, to voice lead smoothly through the progression. Let's take a closer look at the upper-structure block voicings used here:

- In measure 1, the right-hand G minor 7th chord (in 2nd inversion) is built from the 3rd of the overall E♭maj7 chord, upgrading it to an E♭maj9 in total.

- In measure 2, the right-hand C minor 7th chord is built from the 3rd of the overall A♭maj7 chord, upgrading it to an A♭maj9 in total.

- In measure 3, the right-hand F minor 7th chord (in 2nd inversion) is built from the 5th of the overall B♭7sus chord, upgrading it to a B♭9sus in total.

- Measure 4 is similar to measure 1, with the upper Gmi7 voicing now in 1st inversion.

- In measure 5, the right-hand E♭ major 7th chord (in 2nd inversion) is built from the 3rd of the overall Cm7 chord, upgrading it to a Cm9 in total.

- In measure 6, the right-hand A♭ major 7th chord is built from the 3rd of the overall Fm7 chord, upgrading it to an Fm9 in total.

- Measures 7-8 are similar to measures 3-4, with the upper Fmi7 and Gmi7 voicings now in 1st inversion and root position, respectively.

All these voicing choices have upgraded their respective chord symbols, to five-part (or 9th) chords. These are common sounds in classic R&B/pop and ballad styles. Nevertheless, on charts or in fakebooks, we often see only four-part (or 7th) chord symbols, and sometimes even just triad symbols, for songs in this genre. Experienced players often upgrade these more basic chord symbols as desired.

Our next style example uses all the right-hand upper-structure block voicings from Track 18, in a typical R&B ballad comping style.

Classic R&B Style Example #2
Track 19

The right-hand voicings are played on beat 1 of each measure, and are then split up (arpeggiated) during beat 2, leading to a 16th-note anticipation of beat 3. Meanwhile, the left hand is playing a steady quarter-note pattern, except for the 16th-note anticipation of beat 2. These rhythms are typical of classic R&B ballad styles. As is common for most piano ballad styles, you'll need to depress the sustain pedal for the duration of each chord.

Our final classic R&B style example again uses all the right-hand upper-structure block voicings from Track 18, this time in a more up-tempo R&B/funk comping style.

Classic R&B Style Example #3

 Track 20

As before, the voicings are played on beat 1 of each measure, followed by partial voicings (mostly triads and 4th/5th intervals) during the measure; these are derived from the full voicing on beat 1 in each case. The right- and left-hand parts engage in a syncopated 16th-note rhythmic conversation back-and-forth, typical of R&B/ Funk keyboard styles.

CHAPTER 5

COOL JAZZ

Jazz is an American music genre that emerged in the late 19th century, then continued to flourish and develop in the 20th century and beyond. Jazz styles in general are noted for their harmonic sophistication, as well as solo and group improvisation.

Cool Jazz emerged in the 1950s and '60s, as a relatively calm and mellow jazz style that emphasized modern, transparent voicings and modal melodies.

Our first voicing example introduces us to **polychords**, a staple of more sophisticated jazz piano styles. The term polychord literally means "one-chord-over-another;" in other words, both hands are playing different chords at the same time.

To understand these voicings, we also need to introduce the **shape concept**. We define a shape as "a three- or four-note structure containing specific internal intervals." These shapes can then be used individually, or combined together within polychords, to create voicings. By this definition, all commonly used triad and four-part chords, including those already seen in this book, would qualify as shapes.

But—some shapes are not easily or helpfully described using individual chord symbols. A good example of this is a **double-4th** shape, a three-note structure with one perfect-4th interval above another (sometimes referred to as "stacked 4ths"). In Cool Jazz styles, this shape is effective as the left-hand component of a polychord voicing, below a triad as the right-hand component. We'll see this voicing concept at work in the following example.

Cool Jazz Voicing Example #1

Track 21

In the example above, the left-hand voicings above are all double-4th shapes built from the root of each minor 7th chord. The right-hand voicings are all minor triads (in 1st inversion), again built from the root of each minor 7th chord.

For this type of polychord voicing to work, the left hand has to be around the middle C area. If the left hand is much lower, the voicing will be muddy and unusable. If the left hand is too high, the voicing will lack definition and may unduly constrain the right-hand register. Let your ear be the judge!

These voicings all add the 11th to each minor 7th chord, due to the left-hand shapes being used. The 11th is a stable upper extension on the minor 7th chord, and is routinely added in jazz styles.

Our first style example uses the polychord voicings from Track 21, in a mellow Cool Jazz Swing style.

Cool Jazz Style Example #1

🔊 Track 22

These voicings are all played in a **rhythmically concerted** style; in other words, both hands are playing together (apart from some occasional right-hand fills). Remember the Swing-8ths feel when you play this example, a rhythmic device used for most classic jazz styles.

Our next voicing example uses **modal** upper-structure triads in the right hand. Let's review some theory about modes before we proceed.

A **mode** is simply a displaced version of a major scale. For example, a Dorian mode means "a major scale starting from its 2nd degree." Therefore, a D Dorian mode is a C major scale displaced to start on the note D, as D is the 2nd degree of C major. Similarly, an E♭ Dorian mode is a D♭ major scale displaced to start on the note E♭, as E♭ is the 2nd degree of D♭ major, and so on.

The major scale that has been displaced to create the mode is called the **relative major**. So, referencing the above examples: C major is the relative major of the D Dorian mode, and D♭ major is the relative major of the E♭ Dorian mode, and so on.

In jazz and more sophisticated harmony, the Dorian mode is a commonly used scale source for a minor 7th chord; in other words, it can be used as a voicing and improvisation source.

To use modal upper-structure voicings on minor 7th chords, we can select triads from the relative major scale of the Dorian mode in question. We'll see this principle at work in the next voicing example.

Cool Jazz Voicing Example #2

 Track 23

In the first two measures of this example, we see 2nd inversion F major, G major, and Emi triads, all placed over the root note D. These all collectively work to define a big-tent **Dmi7** chord, as all of these triads are diatonic to C major, which is the relative major of D Dorian.

Similarly, in the last two measures we see second inversion Gb major, Ab major, and Fmi triads, all placed over the root note Eb. These work collectively to define a big-tent **Ebmi7** chord, because all these triads are diatonic to Db major, the relative major of Eb Dorian.

Using notes and voicings from the Dorian mode on minor 7th chords in this way is a staple jazz harmony technique. Note that these triads variously add the upper extensions (9th, 11th, and 13th) to each minor 7th chord, normally on the weaker beats (beats 2 and 4) of each measure, returning to more definitive voicings on the strong beats.

Our next style example uses all the modal triad voicings from Track 23, in a recognizable Cool Jazz comping style.

Cool Jazz Style Example #2

Track 24

The left hand is playing the root of each minor 7th chord on beat 1 of each strong measure (measures 1, 3, 5) to define the harmony, then adds a melodic part in between that is an effective counterpoint to the modal right-hand triads. All this is typical of 1950s and '60s Cool Jazz styles.

Our last voicing example returns to the polychord technique we saw earlier, this time using double-4th shapes in both hands. This is a signature sound in mainstream jazz styles.

Cool Jazz Voicing Example #3

Track 25

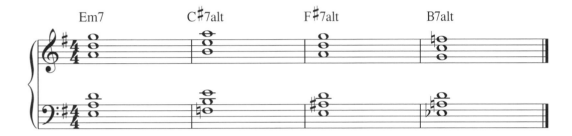

You'll notice the last three chord symbols here have the suffix 7alt. This technically means a dominant 7th chord with any or all possible alterations: ♭5th (aka ♯11th), ♯5th (aka ♭13th), ♭9th, and/or ♯9th. The actual combination of alterations used is left to the player's interpretation. In actual practice, the ♯5th (together with the ♭9th or ♯9th) is often a good default choice in these situations.

Also note that the right-hand double-4th shapes (and the left-hand double-4th in measure 1) all consist of perfect 4th intervals, like the left-hand voicings used in Track 21. However, the last three left-hand voicings here can be considered altered double-4ths, because the bottom interval has been increased to an **augmented 4th** (tritone). This shape is particularly useful for voicing dominant chords, as we can place the 3rd and 7th of the chord, which are a tritone apart, on the bottom of the voicing.

For example, in the left-hand voicings above:

- In measure 2 on the C♯7alt chord, the bottom two notes are F and B, the 3rd and 7th of this chord.
- In measure 3 on the F♯7alt chord, the bottom two notes are E and A♯, the 7th and 3rd of this chord.
- In measure 4 on the B7alt chord, the bottom two notes are D♯ (E♭) and A, the 3rd and 7th of this chord.

Above the 3rd and 7th on these dominant chords, the left-hand thumb is adding an alteration: the ♯9th on the C♯7alt and B7alt chords, and the ♯5th on the F♯7alt chord. So, these voicings could be termed seven-three extended (see Track 1), as we have added another note (an alteration, in this case) to the seven-three voicing in the left hand.

With all this in mind, we can analyze each polychord voicing used in Track 25 as follows:

Measure 1
- The right-hand double-4th is built from the 4th/11th of the overall Em7 chord.
- The left-hand double-4th is built from the root of the overall Em7 chord.

Both of these shapes add the 11th of the chord; as we have seen, this is a stable extension commonly added to the minor 7th chord in jazz styles.

Measure 2
- The right-hand double-4th is built from the 7th of the overall C♯7alt chord, adding two alterations: the ♯9th (E) and ♯5th (A) of the chord.
- The left-hand seven-three extended also adds the ♯9th (E) of the chord.

Measure 3

- The right-hand double-4th is built from the #9th of the overall F#7alt chord, adding three alterations: the #9th (A), the #5th (D), and the ♭9th (G) of the chord.

- The left-hand seven-three extended also adds the #5th (D) of the chord.

Measure 4

- The right-hand double-4th is built from the #5th of the overall B7alt chord, adding three alterations: the #5th (G), the ♭9th (C), and the ♭5th (F) of the chord.

- The left-hand seven-three extended also adds the #9th (D) of the chord.

These right-hand double-4th shapes are a useful way of combining alterations on dominant chords in jazz styles, as you can see! Here's our last style example, which uses these polychord voicings in a medium jazz swing style.

Cool Jazz Style Example #3

 Track 26

In the first half of this example, we're again using concerted rhythms (both hands playing together), similar to earlier jazz examples. In the second half, the right hand is playing some fills over the left-hand voicings, with more of a rhythmic conversation occurring between the hands. The left-hand seven-three extended shapes on the dominant chords, as well as being the lower part of the polychord voicings, are also well-suited to supporting right-hand fills or solo phrases in this way.

For more information on seven-three and seven-three extended voicings, please see *Intro to Jazz Piano* (HL00312088) and *Contemporary Jazz Piano* (HL00311848).

For more information on double-4th shapes, polychord voicings, altered dominant chords, and other advanced theory topics, please see *Contemporary Music Theory, Level Three* (HL00290538).

All titles are published by Hal Leonard.

CHAPTER 6

COUNTRY

Country is an American musical style that emerged in the 1920s and continues to evolve into the 21st century. Traditional country styles normally use basic chord progressions (e.g., I-IV-V) and swing-eighths rhythms, whereas more modern country styles borrow from pop and rock music, with straight-eighths rhythms and more evolved harmonies.

Our first voicing example is in D major and consists of I (D) and IV (G) major triads, with the G major triad inverted to voice lead from the preceding D major chord.

Country Voicing Example #1

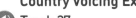 Track 27

There are some manipulations of these triads that are essential to mainstream country styles, so we've shown these in the above example:

- In the first two measures following each basic triad (i.e., measures 3-4 for D major, and 9-10 for G major), we split the right-hand triads into what I call an **alternating-8ths** pattern. The right-hand thumb is playing the bottom note of each triad inversion on the upbeats (halfway through beat 1, halfway through beat 2, etc.), while the upper fingers are playing the remaining triad tones on beats 2 and 4.
- In the next two measures following each basic triad (i.e., measures 5-6 for D major, and 11-12 for G major), we embellish this right-hand alternating-8ths pattern with notes from the respective pentatonic scales: D pentatonic during measures 5-6, and G pentatonic during measures 11-12.

Quick theory review regarding pentatonic scales: D pentatonic contains the notes D-E-F#-A-B; G pentatonic contains the notes G-A-B-D-E. When applying these scales in country styles, we'll often use the tonic or 5th of the scale as a top note (or "drone"), below which other scale tones are played. For example:

- In measures 5-6 above, the top note A (the 5th of D pentatonic) is repeated over other notes from the D pentatonic scale below.
- In measures 11-12 above, the top note G (the root of G pentatonic) is repeated over other notes from the G pentatonic scale below.

Let's put these principles to work in the first style example, in a basic country-pop comping style.

Country Style Example #1

Track 28

This example uses a simple I-IV-V progression in D major. In measures 1-8, we're using the right-hand alternating-8ths triad pattern from Track 27 (measures 3-4 and 9-10). We're also changing triad inversions during each chord (i.e., switching D major triad inversions between measures 1 and 2) to create movement and interest.

Then in measures 9-16, the right hand switches to octave-doubled triads for a more powerful effect. This involves doubling or duplicating one of the right-hand triad tones (either the root, 3rd, or 5th) an octave apart, on the top and bottom of the triad.

- For example, in measure 9, the D major triad is voiced with four notes (A-D-F♯-A from bottom to top), then the bottom note A is split off to create the alternating-8ths pattern, still leaving three notes (the full triad) to land on beats 2 and 4 of the measure.
- Similarly, in measure 11, the G major triad is voiced with four notes (D-G-B-D from bottom to top), then the bottom note D is split off to create the alternating-8ths pattern, and so on.

Right-hand octave-doubled triads are useful in other contemporary styles as well as country music, as we will see.

Our next style example embellishes the previous example in D major, with some of the pentatonic scale techniques introduced with the voicings in Track 27.

Country Style Example #2

 Track 29

This example has the same progression and form as Track 28, now adding the pentatonic scale fills and drone notes from Track 27 (measures 5-6 and 11-12). This would be suitable for a more contemporary country-rock sound.

Our next voicing example is in G major and introduces us to country **walkups** and **walkdowns**. These are often used to connect between chords whose roots are a perfect 4th interval apart—G major to C major and back again, in this example. You'll see that the right hand uses two-note voicings which can be referred to as dyads over a single-note left-hand part:

Country Voicing Example #2

Track 30

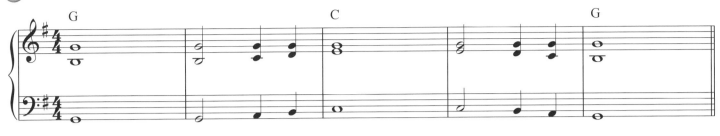

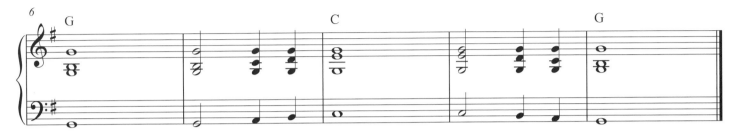

The country walkup and walkdown has three basic components:

- A single-note bass line that "walks up" the major scale of the key, to connect between the chords, played with the left hand
- A parallel line moving a 10th interval (octave plus a 3rd) above the bass line, played with the right hand
- A drone (repeated top note), also played with the right hand: normally the root of the chord when walking up, and the 5th of the chord when walking down.

In measures 1-5 above, we see these three elements at work, creating a basic walkup from the G major to the C major chord, and a walkdown from the C major back to the G major chord. Then in measures 6-10, we have the same sequence, but now with octave doubling in the right hand (doubling the drone (top note), one octave lower) to create a bigger, more powerful sound.

Our last style example uses these walkups and walkdowns in a traditional Swing-8ths rhythmic style, with some pentatonic fills added.

Country Style Example #3

Track 31

In comparison to the basic walkup and walkdown voicings from Track 30, note that we've added some eighth-note subdivision in the right hand (in the even-numbered measures). This is played by the right-hand thumb (an octave below the drone note) on all the upbeats (halfway through beat 1, halfway through beat 2, etc.). We saw this octave doubling of the drone note, in measures 6-10 of Track 30.

All of this creates a traditional country comping style, although we do have some contemporary touches with the brief pentatonic fills at the end of the odd-numbered measures. (See Track 27 comments.)

CHAPTER 7

FUNK

Funk music emerged in the 1970s, as an earthy and highly rhythmic variant of R&B. This style has a big emphasis on groove and syncopation, and piano and keyboards frequently play an important role.

Our first voicing example is in E minor and uses a device I refer to as **minor pentatonic 4th intervals** in my books and classes. We'll need to review a little theory here, to make sure we understand this concept.

The E minor pentatonic scale contains the notes E-G-A-B-D. If we measure intervals up from the tonic (E) to the other notes in the scale, we get: minor 3rd, perfect 4th, perfect 5th, and minor 7th intervals respectively. This scale is also the same as a G pentatonic (sometimes referred to as a G major pentatonic) scale, but repositioned to start on the note E (the relative minor of G major).

The voicings shown below use all the perfect 4th intervals available internally within this E minor pentatonic scale, then place these intervals over different root notes available within the key of E minor. Why perfect 4ths? Well, these intervals have a hollow transparent sound that is quite suited to funk (and some rock) styles.

This concept of floating various minor pentatonic 4th intervals over root notes available within the same minor key is used in many funk and rock songs. (Stevie Wonder's "Superstition" is one of the most famous examples.)

So, let's take a look at these voicings, using perfect 4th intervals from the E minor pentatonic scale, over various chord roots available in the key of E minor.

Funk Voicing Example #1

 Track 32

These voicings add various unaltered upper extensions to the chord symbols shown, for example:
- In measure 1, the 11th is added to the Emi7 chord.
- In measure 2, the 6th and 9th are added to the Cmaj7 chord.
- In measure 3, the 6th and 9th are added to the Dsus chord.
- In measure 1, the 7th and 9th are added to the Asus chord.

These upper extensions would normally be acceptable in all but the most basic funk and modern rock styles.

You should also be aware of the functions of these chord symbols, with respect to the overall key of E minor. For example:
- In measure 1, the Emi7 is a I (tonic) chord, in the key of E minor.
- In measure 2, the Cmaj7 is a ♭VI (flat 6) chord, in the key of E minor.
- In measure 3, the Dsus is a ♭VII (flat 7) chord, in the key of E minor.
- In measure 4, the Asus is a IV (four) chord, in the key of E minor.

These functions are common in minor keys, so being acquainted with them will facilitate transposing songs/progressions into other keys—and is recommended for your musicianship in general.

Next, we'll apply these voicings in a 16th-note funk comping style.

Funk Style Example #1

 Track 33

The chord symbols in this example are the same as for Track 32. For this type of funk comping style, I recommend creating the right-hand rhythmic pattern first, then fitting in the left hand in the rhythmic spaces (between the right hand). Here, the right hand is anticipating (landing ahead of) beat 3 by a 16th-note, (i.e., landing on the last 16th of beat 2, followed by a rest on beat 3).

Meanwhile, the left hand is often landing a 16th-note ahead of a right-hand voicing, functioning as a rhythmic pickup into the right hand, which creates forward motion and a funky quality. All this is typical of 16th-note funk comping styles.

This overall approach is effective for funky clavinet and staccato organ stylings, as well as electric and acoustic piano sounds.

Our next style example uses these same voicing techniques, this time in a Swing-8ths funky shuffle style.

Funk Style Example #2

Track 34

Just a quick hint on interpreting the notation above:

As seen in some earlier examples, the Swing-8ths text above the staff tells us to divide each pair of eighth notes in a two-thirds/one-third ratio; this is equivalent to using the first and third eighth-notes only, within an eighth-note triplet.

However, we also see some eighth-note triplet signs in this example. This is solely for the purpose of accessing the middle (second) event in the eighth-note triplet – which the Swing-8ths feel would not normally use.

So, all the eighth notes that are not under triplet signs, you'll interpret as swing 8ths, as usual. But, when you see the eighth-note triplet signs, be aware that we're accessing the middle (second) event as above.

Have a listen to Track 34, to get familiar with this important rhythmic concept.

Again, the right-hand rhythmic phrase here is driving the groove, with the left-hand thumb note fitting in between the rhythmic spaces available.

Our next voicing example is in the key of C minor, and introduces some half-step interval movements common in classic funk styles.

Funk Voicing Example #2

Track 35

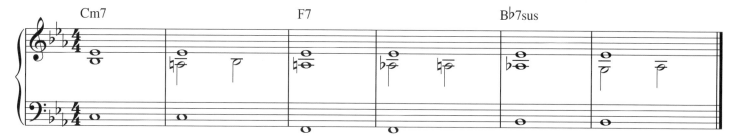

The above voicing example can be divided into two-measure phrases, as follows:

Measures 1-2

- In measure 1, we have a seven-three voicing in the right hand, for the Cm7 chord; in other words, we're playing just the 7th and 3rd of the chord (see Chapters 1 and 11).

- In measure 2, the note A is moving (resolving) to the note B♭, within the Cm7 chord. This is technically a 13th moving to the 7th within the chord.

Measures 3-4

- In measure 3, we have a seven-three voicing in the right hand, for the F7 chord.

- In measure 4, the note A♭ is moving (resolving) to the note A, within the F7 chord. This is technically a #9th (sharped 9th) moving to the 3rd within the chord.

Measures 5-6

- In measure 5, we have a seven-four voicing in the right hand, for the B♭7sus chord; the 4th has replaced the 3rd in this case, as the chord is suspended.

- In measure 6, the note G is moving or resolving to the note A♭, within the B♭7sus chord. This is technically a 13th moving to the 7th within the chord.

Our last style example uses these half-step voicing movements, within a classic swing-16ths funk groove.

Funk Style Example #3

Track 36

Note the Swing-16ths text shown above the music: instead of the 16th notes dividing half-a-beat exactly in half, this is divided in a two-thirds/one-third ratio. This is equivalent to playing each pair of 16th-notes as an eighth-note/16th-note triplet, and is common in funk and hip-hop/R&B styles. Check out the audio track to get comfortable with this important Swing-16ths feel.

In addition to the voicings shown in Track 35, we also see upper-structure triad voicings on the Bb7sus chord (F minor and Ab major triads built from the 5th and 7th, respectively).

CHAPTER 8

GOSPEL

Gospel originated in African-American churches in the early 20th century—combining hymns, spiritual songs, and Southern folk music. Gospel, together with blues and country music, created the foundation for rock'n'roll styles, beginning in the 1950s. Gospel music has a distinctive keyboard vocabulary, which can be used to enhance your contemporary rock and R&B stylings.

Our first voicing example is in G major, and uses **modal** upper-structure triads in the right hand, similar to the example in Track 23; now, however, we're using triads from Mixolydian modes instead of Dorian modes.

Quick review: As we saw in Chapter 5, a mode is a displaced version of a major scale. Here, a Mixolydian mode means "a major scale starting from its 5th degree." So, a G Mixolydian mode is a C major scale displaced to start on the note G, since G is the 5th degree of C major. The C major scale can therefore be termed the relative major of the G Mixolydian mode.

The Mixolydian mode is a commonly used scale source for a **dominant 7th** chord. Therefore, to use modal upper-structure voicings on dominant 7th chords, we'll select triads from the relative major scale of the Mixolydian mode that correspond to each dominant 7th chord. We'll see this principle at work in the next voicing example.

Gospel Voicing Example #1

 Track 37

In the first measure of this example, we see 2nd-inversion B diminished, D minor, and C major triads in the right hand, all placed over left-hand intervals with the root note of G on the bottom. These voicings work collectively to define a big-tent G7 dominant chord, as all of the upper triads are diatonic to C major, the relative major of G Mixolydian.

Similarly, in the second measure we see 2nd-inversion E diminished, G minor, and F major triads in the right hand, all placed over left-hand intervals with the root note of C on the bottom. These voicings work collectively to define a big-tent C7 dominant chord, as all of the upper triads are diatonic to F major, the relative major of C Mixolydian.

Finally, in the third measure we see 2nd-inversion F♯ diminished, A minor, and G major triads in the right hand, all placed over left-hand intervals with the root note of D on the bottom. These voicings work collectively to define a big-tent D7 dominant chord, as all of the upper triads are diatonic to G major, the relative major of D Mixolydian.

Using voicings from Mixolydian modes on dominant 7th chords in this way is a staple gospel and blues harmony technique. Note that these triads variously add upper extensions (11th and 13th) to each dominant 7th chord, normally on the weaker beats of each measure (beats 2 and 4), returning to more definitive voicings on the strong beats.

The left-hand voicings here use a mix of root-5th, root-6th (13th), and root-7th intervals, to complement and reinforce the top notes of the right-hand voicings.

Our first style example uses all the modal triad voicings from Track 37, in a 3/4 (three beats per measure) Classic Gospel comping style.

Gospel Style Example #1

Track 38

This traditional gospel comping style has three beats per measure, and uses a Swing-8ths rhythmic subdivision.

Note that the left and right hands are playing concerted (rhythmically synchronized) rhythms. This is typical for the style.

Our next voicing example is in the key of A major, and uses internal IV-I triad movements (sometimes referred to as **backcycling** in gospel circles).

Gospel Voicing Example #2

Track 39

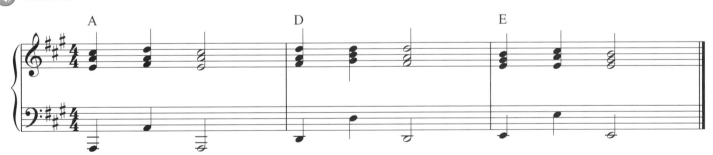

Each measure in the above voicing example can be analyzed as follows:

Measure 1

The right-hand triads are moving from A major (in 2nd inversion) to D major (in 1st inversion), and back again, all over the root note of A in the left hand (using an octave pattern). We could have written these chord symbols as A to D/A, and back to A, and you will see this written in charts sometimes.

However, the upper D major triad is actually used as a passing shape to provide movement between the A major triads in this measure. For that reason, players will typically add this interior triad movement—in the right stylistic circumstances—even if, as in this case, we see only the basic A major triad chord symbol on the chart.

Measure 2

We see the same situation on the D major chord. The right-hand triads are moving between D major and G major, and back again; however, we see only the D chord symbol for the whole measure.

Measure 3

Similarly, the right-hand triads are moving between E major and A major, and back again; however, we see only the E chord symbol for the whole measure.

We've seen this type of IV-I upper-triad movement before, on Track 14 in Chapter 3 (Classic Rock). As well as being typical of gospel styles, this harmonic device is widely used in blues and blues-rock styles (for example, in numerous Rolling Stones songs).

Our next style example uses these backcycled triad movements, to voice an up-tempo contemporary gospel groove.

Gospel Style Example #2

 Track 40

Each of the above I, IV and V chords in A major, is using the backcycled triad movement (internal I-IV and back again) shown in Track 39.

Here, the left hand is playing a steady eighth-note octave pattern typical of fast gospel styles, which provides an effective foundation below the 16th-note rhythms and anticipations in the right hand.

Our final style example is a variation on Track 40, now with different rhythms and octave-doubled triads in the right hand, over a mix of eighth- and 16th-note rhythms in the left hand.

Gospel Style Example #3

 Track 41

In comparing this to Track 40, we see that the right-hand triads are octave-doubled, with one of the upper triad tones duplicated on the top and bottom of the voicing. (See comments for Track 28.)

In the left hand, to vary the continuous eighth-note octaves from Track 40, we now see some 16th/dotted-eighth beamed pairs of notes. These are normally followed by a right-hand triad on the following upbeat. For example, in measure 1 the 16th/dotted-eighth figure starting on beat 4 in the left hand is immediately followed by a triad halfway through beat 4 (& of 4) in the right hand.

This type of rhythmic pickup, a left-hand figure leading into the right-hand triad, is a signature sound in up-tempo gospel styles.

CHAPTER 9

HIP-HOP

Hip-Hop is a music genre that uses a rhythmic style of speaking (rapping), over backing tracks and beats. This style originated in the 1970s, and its popularity continues into the 21st century, exerting a significant influence on today's rock and R&B productions.

Hip-Hop song forms are often basic and repetitive; for example, taking a simple two-measure or four-measure phrase and repeating it throughout the whole song. The style predominantly uses triad voicings, with occasional suspensions and larger chords.

Our first voicing example shows a diatonic triad progression in the key of B♭.

Hip-Hop Voicing Example #1

Track 42

Here, we see major triads and one minor triad in the right hand, placed over root notes in the left hand. All these triads are found within (are diatonic to) the key of B♭ major. Triad inversions are used to voice lead smoothly between the chords. It should be pointed out, however, that Hip-Hop styles don't always use voice leading; see the next voicing example.

Our first style example uses the triad voicings from Track 42, in a typical mid-tempo Hip-Hop style.

Hip-Hop Style Example #1

Track 43

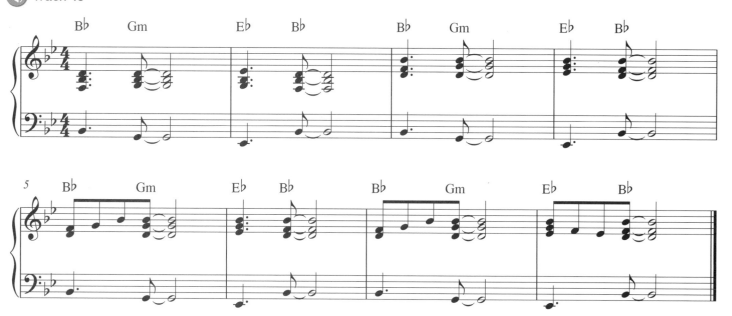

In measures 1-2, the voicings are the same as in Track 42, now with the second chord in each measure landing ahead of (anticipating) beat 3. This pattern is repeated in measures 3-4, with different right-hand triad inversions to voice lead in a higher register.

Then, in measures 5, 7, and 8, we're adding simple eighth-note pentatonic fills to connect between the right-hand triads. These fills are derived from the B♭ and E♭ pentatonic scales.

Our next voicing example uses basic minor triads in the right hand, placed over chord roots in the left hand. Note that these simple voicings don't use inversions to voice lead (move closely) from one chord to the next; rather, we're simply moving between 2nd-inversion triads "in parallel." In Hip-Hop and other computer-based electronic music styles, this is sometimes the result of manipulating and transposing loops or samples, rather than the part actually being played when recording.

Hip-Hop Voicing Example #2

Track 44

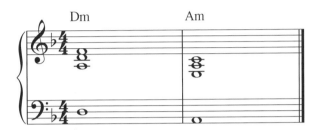

Our next style example uses the minor-triad voicings from Track 44, with sparse keyboard rhythms.

Hip-Hop Style Example #2

Track 45

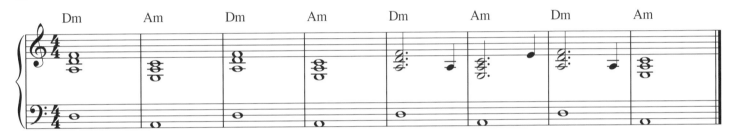

The backing track for this example uses a mid-tempo eighth-note rhythmic feel, with just a hint of Swing-16ths rhythmic subdivision in the bass and kick drum parts. (See Track 36 and its accompanying text.) Over this rhythm section, the piano part above is minimal and straightforward – just whole-note rhythms in measures 1-4, then adding a simple quarter-note pickup in measures 5-7. This type of piano part is more of a harmonic background part, and doesn't add any rhythmic information to the track.

Our last voicing example uses a mix of **sus2** chords and triads, in the key of B minor.

Hip-Hop Voicing Example #3

Track 46

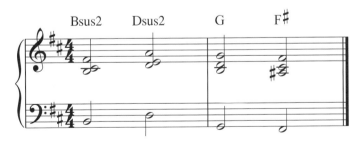

Here we see a mix of sus2 and major triads in the right hand, placed over root notes in the left hand. The sus2 symbol means we have replaced the 3rd of the chord with the "2," which is a whole-step above the root; it is also the 9th of the chord in question. This creates a modern texture often used in today's rock and R&B styles.

Another way to look at the voicings in measure 1: they are both inverted double-4th shapes built from the 9th of each chord. In Chapter 5, we were introduced to double-4th shapes, as three-note structures with one perfect 4th interval on top of another. Well, if we take a C#-F#-B double-4th and invert it so that F# is on top, we get the voicing shown at the start of the first measure above. In other words, we've built a double-4th from the 9th of the Bsus2 chord. Similar logic applies to the Dsus2 chord in measure 1.

Our last style example takes the voicings from Track 46, and applies a driving quarter-note rhythmic pattern in a more up-tempo hip-hop style.

Hip-Hop Style Example #3
Track 47

In measures 1-4, the right hand is playing steady quarter-note voicings that help to drive the groove. The left hand is playing the root of each chord on beats 1 and 3, adding eighth-note pickups into these downbeats.

In measures 5-8, the right hand gets a little busier with arpeggios (playing the notes of the chord one-at-a-time) during beat 2 of each measure. Meanwhile, the left-hand thumb is playing some eighth-note pickups to add rhythmic motion to the groove.

CHAPTER 10

JAZZ FUSION

Jazz Fusion originated in the 1960s by combining jazz harmony and improvisation with the rock rhythms and instrumentation emerging at the time. Fusion was then a precursor to the various Contemporary Jazz sub-styles from the 1980s onward, which added significant R&B and Funk elements to the stylistic mix.

Our first voicing example uses a mix of triad, double-4th, and block (four-part) shapes in the right hand, over various root-11th, root-7th, root-3rd, and root-note voicings in the left hand.

Jazz Fusion Voicing Example #1

 Track 48

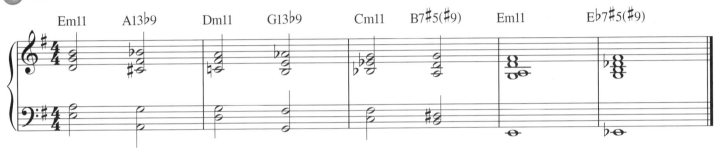

You'll notice that these chord symbols are more detailed compared to earlier voicing examples, with more upper extensions and alterations shown. This example contains several altered dominant chord symbols (dominant chords with altered 5ths and/or altered 9ths).

Adding extensions (i.e., 9th and 13th) and alterations (i.e., ♭5th, #5th, ♭9th, #9th) to dominant chords, is a major harmony topic; we devote several chapters to the topic in our *Contemporary Music Theory, Level Three* book. However, here are some introductory comments to get you started on the examples in this chapter.

- We've already seen voicing examples with basic dominant-chord symbols (e.g., C7, F7) in this book, where unaltered extensions such as 9th and 13th have been added in the corresponding style examples. (See Chapter 1.) This is routine in blues, jazz, and gospel styles.

- The dominant chord alterations seen above are more advanced and sophisticated. However, jazz musicians may still add them in response to basic dominant chord symbols, if the style and context permits.

- For now, to help introduce us to these more sophisticated dominant chord sounds, we've shown more detailed chord symbols; these specify the extensions/alterations throughout Track 48.

- Although you'll often see these symbols in better jazz fakebooks, remember that the whole treatment of dominant-chord harmony is subject to interpretation and preference.

Bearing all this in mind, let's analyze each voicing used in Track 48:

Measure 1, Beat 1
- The right-hand G major triad is built from the 3rd of the overall Em11 chord.
- The left hand is playing a root-11th or root-4th interval.

This combination of left- and right-hand voicings creates interlocking double-4th shapes: E-A-D and A-D-G (built from the root and 11th of the minor chord, respectively).

Measure 1, Beat 3
- The right-hand F# major triad is built from the 13th of the overall A13(♭9) chord; this adds the 13th and ♭9th to the dominant chord.
- The left hand is playing a root-7th interval.

Measure 2, Beat 1

- The right-hand F major triad is built from the 3rd of the overall Dm11 chord.
- The left hand is playing a root-11th or root-4th interval.

This combination of left- and right-hand voicings creates interlocking double-4th shapes: D-G-C and G-C-F (built from the root and 11th of the minor chord, respectively).

Measure 2, Beat 3

- The right-hand E major triad is built from the 13th of the overall G13(♭9) chord; this adds the 13th and ♭9th to the dominant chord.
- The left hand is playing a root-7th interval.

Measure 3, Beat 1

- The right-hand E♭ major triad is built from the 3rd of the overall Cm11 chord.
- The left hand is playing a root-11th or root-4th interval.

This combination of left- and right-hand voicings creates interlocking double-4th shapes: C-F-B♭ and F-B♭-E♭ (built from the root and 11th of the minor chord, respectively).

Measure 3, Beat 3

- The right-hand double-4th A-D-G is built from the 7th of the overall B7(#5, #9) chord; this adds the #9th and #5th to the dominant chord.
- The left hand is playing a root-3rd interval.

Here, for the note D to sound like a sharped 9th, the 3rd (D# in this case) is also needed in the voicing; hence, the root-3rd interval in the left hand. This will be muddy if played too low; this example is near the bottom of the useful range.

Measure 4

The right-hand shape here is a hybrid (combination) of two three-note shapes:

- The top three notes (A-D-F#) are a 2nd-inversion D major triad, built from the 7th of the Em11 chord.
- The bottom three notes (G-A-D) are an inverted double-4th (A-D-G in root position), built from the 4th/11th of the Em11 chord.

Meanwhile, the left hand is playing the root of the chord (E).

Measure 5

- The right-hand four-part block shape (Gma7♭5) is built from the 3rd of the overall E♭7(#5,#9) chord; this adds the #9th and #5th to the dominant chord.
- The left hand is playing the root (Eb).

We saw upper-structure block (four-part) shapes used earlier in Chapter 4. Here we're using an altered block shape (major 7th with ♭5th), built from the 3rd of the overall dominant chord. Altered major 7th block shapes are highly useful upper-structures in jazz styles.

Our first style example uses the upper-structure voicings from Track 48, in a funky 16th-note Jazz Fusion style.

Jazz Fusion Style Example #1

 Track 49

In measures 1-6, the voicings are all played in a rhythmically concerted style, with both hands playing together. Then, starting in measure 7, we have a funkier rhythmically alternating comping style between the hands, similar to the earlier Funk example in Track 33.

Our next voicing example is in G major, and uses Mixolydian modal upper-structure triads in the right hand – similar to the example in Track 37, except that now we're using 1st-inversion triads instead of 2nd-inversion triads.

We've seen before that the Mixolydian mode is a commonly used scale source for a dominant 7th chord. In the next voicing example, we're using 1st-inversion triads from various Mixolydian modes, as follows:

- Measures 1-2 on the G7 chord: all triads are from G Mixolydian (C major).
- Measures 3-4 on the Bb7 chord: all triads are from Bb Mixolydian (Eb major).
- Measures 5-6 on the C7 chord: all triads are from C Mixolydian (F major).

Jazz Fusion Voicing Example #2

Track 50

In measures 1-2 of this example, we see 1st-inversion E minor, D minor, and F major triads in the right hand, all placed over the left-hand root note of G. These voicings work collectively to define a big-tent G7 dominant chord.

In measures 3-4 of this example, we see 1st-inversion G minor, F minor, and A♭ major triads in the right hand, all placed over the left-hand root note of B♭. These voicings work collectively to define a big-tent B♭7 dominant chord.

In measures 5-6 of this example, we see 1st-inversion A minor, G minor, and B♭ major triads in the right hand, all placed over the left-hand root note of C. These voicings work collectively to define a big-tent C7 dominant chord.

Our next style example uses all the modal triad voicings from Track 50, in a Jazz Fusion Shuffle comping style.

Jazz Fusion Style Example #2

Track 51

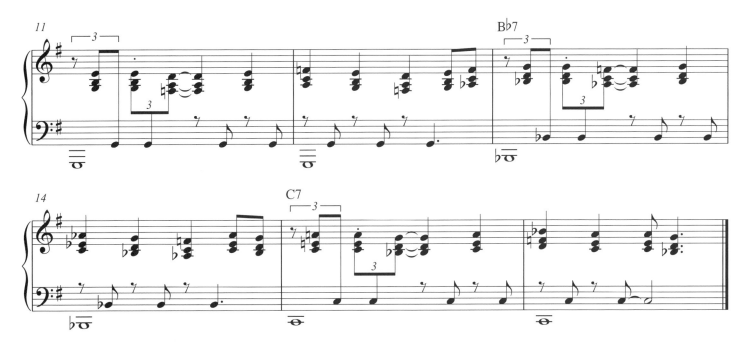

Note this this example has a Swing-8ths feel, and yet there are some occasional eighth-note triplet signs in the music, enabling us to access the middle event of the eighth-note triplet. (See the text following Track 34.)

Our last style example again uses the modal triad voicings from Track 50, this time in a Swing-16ths (Funk Shuffle) comping style.

Jazz Fusion Style Example #3

 Track 52

Note the Swing-16ths text above the music; review text following Track 36 as needed. This example again features a rhythmic conversation between the hands, typical of funk and jazz fusion styles.

CHAPTER 11

JAZZ SWING

Jazz Swing refers a to classic, straight-ahead jazz style that originated in the 1930s and '40s; it is still a strong presence in mainstream jazz today. Many "standard" songs—which became part of the Great American Songbook—were written during this period. They were then interpreted in the Swing styles of the era.

Our first voicing example uses block voicings on the **II-V-I** chord progression; these are a staple of mainstream jazz and "standard" tunes. The term II-V-I refers to chords built from the 2nd, 5th, and tonic (1st) degrees of the key, respectively. In jazz tunes, you'll normally see these progressions written with four-part (7th) chord symbols.

Jazz Swing Voicing Example #1

🔊 Track 53

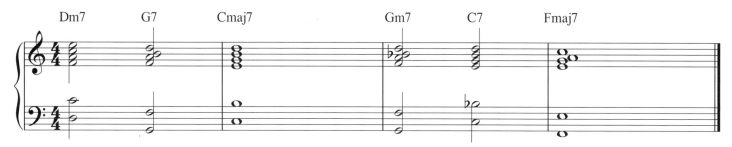

This progression consists of a II-V-I in C major (measures 1-2), followed by a II-V-I in F major (measures 3-4). This is a typical sequence in jazz swing styles.

Note that we have used upper-structure block (4-part) voicings on each chord, similar to the treatment in the Blues Chapter for Track 4. Now, however, we are voicing different types of chords (minor, dominant, and major), not just dominant chords.

Let's look at the above voicing choices in more detail:

- For the minor 7th chords (Dm7 in measure 1 and Gm7 in measure 3), we're building major 7th block shapes from the 3rd of each chord. This upgrades both of the minor 7th chords to minor 9th chords.

- For the dominant 7th chords (G7 in measure 1 and C7 in measure 3), we're building minor 7th (♭5) block shapes from the 3rd of each chord. This upgrades both of the dominant 7th chords to dominant 9th chords. (This is the voicing technique used in Track 4.)

- For the major 7th chords (Cmaj7 in measure 2 and Fmaj7 in measure 4), we're building minor 7th block shapes from the 3rd of each chord. This upgrades both of the major 7th chords to major 9th chords.

As a result of using these upper-structure block voicings, the right hand is playing the 3rd, 5th, 7th, and 9th of each chord. In straight-ahead jazz and swing styles, this type of harmonic upgrade is routinely done in response to the basic (four-part) chord symbols shown in Track 53.

In the left hand, we are playing the root and 7th of each chord, which gives definitive support below the right-hand voicings, and is a typical jazz sound. Don't play root-7th intervals too low on the keyboard, or they will sound muddy; let your ear be the judge.

Our next style example uses the upper-structure block voicings from Track 53, in a classic Jazz Swing style.

Jazz Swing Style Example #1

Track 54

In measures 1-8, the voicings are all played in a rhythmically concerted style; in other words, both hands are playing together. Then from measure 9 onward, the left-hand pinky plays and holds the root of each chord on beat 1, while the thumb plays the 7th with the same rhythms as the right-hand voicings. This is an effective comping variation in basic swing styles.

Don't forget the Swing-8ths feel when you play this example, as noted at the top of the chart.

Our next voicing example is a variation on the polychord (one-chord-above-another) technique we saw earlier, using the same block shapes from Tracks 53-54—but this time in the left hand, around the middle C area. Above that, in the right hand, we're using a device I refer to as **filled-in octaves** in my books and classes.

A filled-in octave is simply an octave interval with another note inside (or in between). The doubled note, and the added note in between, will need to be valid functions on the chord in question, of course. Favorite choices in jazz styles are the 7-3 (7th and 3rd), as well as other chord tones such as 9-5 (9th and 5th).

In the following example, we've used filled-in octaves with 9ths and 5ths in the right hand, over block shapes in the left hand; these are the same as the right-hand voicings from Track 53, but an octave lower.

Jazz Swing Voicing Example #2

Track 55

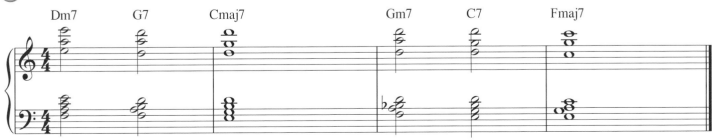

As with all polychord-type voicings, you should ensure that the left-hand shape is in the middle C area, not too high or too low. Here, this pushes the right-hand filled-in octave voicings up to the top of the treble staff and above. These voicings have clarity and projection in this higher register.

Our next style example uses the polychord-type voicings from Track 56, in a more up-tempo Jazz Swing style.

Jazz Swing Style Example #2

 Track 56

In measures 1-8, and 9-16, we see two different sets of concerted rhythms used between the hands. All this is idiomatic for Jazz Swing comping styles.

Our last voicing example again uses the polychord technique, this time using a mix of triads, double-4ths, and block shapes in the right hand, combined with double-4ths (or altered double-4ths) in the left hand. This is a highly useful combination in straight-ahead jazz styles.

Jazz Swing Voicing Example #3

Track 57

As seen in Track 48, some of the dominant-chord symbols here show specific alterations (A7#5#9, Bb13b9, etc.), which are voiced accordingly. For the other dominant chord symbols, as well as the major and minor 7th chords, we have added some unaltered upper extensions, 9th and/or 13th, which are appropriate for this style.

Also, as seen in Track 48, we're using some altered double-4ths as left-hand voicings on the dominant chords; these all have the 7-3 (7th and 3rd) of the dominant chord on the bottom. We're also using an altered double-4th as a left-hand voicing on the Em7(b5) chord; this time, the tritone interval on the bottom is the root and b5th of the chord. All of these voicings are characteristic mainstream jazz sounds.

With all this in mind, we can analyze each polychord voicing used in Track 57 as follows:

Measure 1
- The right-hand G minor triad is built from the 3rd of the overall Em7(b5) chord.
- The left-hand altered double-4th contains the root, b5th, and 7th of the chord.

Measure 2
- The right-hand F major triad is built from the #5th (b13th) of the overall A13(#5#9) chord; this adds the #5th and #9th to the dominant chord.
- The left hand seven-three extended shape also adds the #5th (b13th) of the chord (F).

Measure 3
- The right-hand Eb major triad is built from the 3rd of the overall Cm11 chord.
- The left-hand double-4th is built from the 5th of the chord, which adds the 11th (F).

This combination of left- and right-hand voicings creates interlocking double-4th shapes: C-F-Bb and F-Bb-Eb (built from the root and 11th of the minor chord, respectively).

Measure 4
- The right-hand double-4th is built from the 9th of the overall F7 chord.
- The left-hand seven-three extended shape also adds the 13th of the chord (D).

This combination of left- and right-hand voicings creates interlocking double-4th shapes: A-D-G and D-G-C (built from the 3rd and 13th of the dominant chord, respectively).

Measure 5
- The right-hand Abmaj7 block shape is built from the 3rd of the overall Fm7 chord.
- The left-hand double-4th is built from the root of the chord, which adds the 11th (Bb).

Measure 6
- The right-hand G major triad is built from the 13th of the overall Bb13(b9) chord; this adds the 13th and b9th to the dominant chord.
- The left-hand seven-three extended shape also adds the 13th of the chord (G).

Measure 7
- The right-hand Bb major triad (with octave doubling) is built from the 5th of the overall Ebmaj7 chord.
- The left-hand double-4th is built from the 3rd of the chord, which adds the 6th (C) and 9th (F).

Measure 8

- The right-hand double-4th is built from the 3rd of the overall Ab7 chord, this adds the 13th (F) and the 9th (Bb) to the dominant chord.
- The left-hand seven-three extended shape also adds the 13th of the chord (F).

These chord changes are typically used for the first eight measures of the famous standard "Stella by Starlight," which virtually all jazz musicians will play at some point in their careers. Here's a typical Jazz Swing rhythmic treatment of these voicings.

Jazz Swing Style Example #3

Track 58

Again, this example mostly uses concerted rhythms (both hands playing together), with some triad splits and left-hand pickups in the second half. This should help prepare you for your first (or next) gig playing from *The Real Book* (HL00240221), a commonly-used fake book of jazz charts and standards!

> For more information on double-4th shapes, polychord voicings, altered dominant chords, and other advanced theory topics, please see *Contemporary Music Theory, Level Three* (HL00290538), published by Hal Leonard.

CHAPTER 12

MODERN ROCK

Modern Rock is something of a catch-all term encompassing contemporary rock and pop styles from the 21st century. Compared to most Classic Rock from the 20th century (see Chapter 3), the chord voicings are often sparser and more open-sounding. Piano and keyboards often play an important role.

Our first voicing example is in A major, with some chords borrowed from A minor. This mix of major and minor keys from the same tonic (A, in this case) is common in the more evolved modern rock styles. Here, the right-hand voicings are all filled-in octaves, an octave interval with one other note inside (or within the octave). This is a useful technique across a range of contemporary piano styles.

We also see that the top and bottom notes of the octave intervals are A (the tonic of the key) throughout, and that the filled-in notes in between, are either D or E. This all combines to create a series of open, transparent 4th and 5th intervals in the right hand—a powerful sound suited to modern Rock styles.

These filled-in octaves (with the interior 4th and 5th intervals) are then placed over various chord roots available in the keys of A major and A minor (i.e., A, F, D, and G). We've used more detailed chord symbols here, to reflect the use of these right-hand shapes over the different root notes; however, you could apply these voicings to more basic chord symbols to get this stylistic effect.

Modern Rock Voicing Example #1

🔊 Track 59

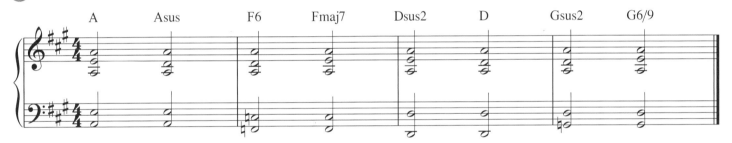

These right-hand voicings add various suspensions or extensions to the overall chords, as follows:

Measure 1, Beat 1
- The right-hand A-E-A filled-in octave is the root and 5th of the A chord, sometimes referred to as a power-chord voicing (root and 5th only).

Measure 1, Beat 3
- The right-hand A-D-A filled-in octave is the root and 4th of the A chord, creating an Asus voicing (the 4th replacing the 3rd of the chord in this case).
- The left hand is playing a root-5th interval below each of the above voicings.

Measure 2, Beat 1
- The right-hand A-D-A filled-in octave is the 3rd and 6th of the F chord, creating an F6 or Fmaj6 voicing in total.

Measure 2, Beat 3
- The right-hand A-E-A filled-in octave is the 3rd and 7th of the F chord, creating an Fmaj7 voicing in total.
- The left hand is playing a root-5th interval below each of the above voicings.

Measure 3, Beat 1

- The right-hand A-E-A filled-in octave is the 5th and 9th of the D chord, creating a Dsus2 voicing (the 2nd (or 9th) replacing the 3rd of the chord in this case).

Measure 3, Beat 3

- The right-hand A-D-A filled-in octave is the 5th and root of the D chord, sometimes referred to as a power-chord voicing (root and 5th only).
- The left hand is playing the root in octaves, below each of the above voicings.

Measure 4, Beat 1

- The right-hand A-D-A filled-in octave is the 9th and 5th of the G chord, creating a Gsus2 voicing (the 2nd (or 9th) replacing the 3rd of the chord in this case).

Measure 4, Beat 3

- The right-hand A-E-A filled-in octave is the 9th and 6th of the G chord, implying a G6/9 (G major 6/9) voicing in total.
- The left hand is playing a root-5th interval below each of the above voicings.

These upper extensions would normally be acceptable in more evolved modern rock styles.

Now let's apply these voicings in a driving eighth-note rock comping groove.

Modern Rock Style Example #1

 Track 60

In the first eight measures, we see both hands playing concerted rhythms with typical eighth-note anticipations. Then in the second eight measures, the right hand builds the energy level with continuous eighth-note voicings.

Note that some of the chord symbols are written directly on the rhythmic anticipations (upbeats). If you listen to the backing track, you'll hear that this matches up with the anticipations in the rhythm section.

Our next voicing example is again in the key of A, and uses triads and suspensions common in modern rock styles.

Modern Rock Voicing Example #2

Track 61

For each measure in this example, we move from a basic major triad voicing to a suspended triad, and then back again. Here the term suspended triad means we are replacing the 3rd of the chord with the 4th, the note a perfect 4th interval above the root of the chord.

For example, in the first measure on beat 1, the right hand is playing a root-position A major triad. Then on beat 2, the 3rd of the chord (C#) is replaced with the 4th (D), creating the Asus chord. Then on beat 3, the suspension resolves back to the A major triad again. Similar movements occur within the G major triad in measure 2, and the (inverted) D major triad in measure 3.

Although the suspensions here are reflected in the chord symbols, players may sometimes improvise these interior harmonic movements within a more basic chord structure, if the style and context permit.

Our next style example uses these triad suspensions and resolutions, within a modern Swing-16ths Rock style.

Modern Rock Style Example #2

🔊 Track 62

Note the Swing-16ths text above the music; review the text following Track 36 as needed.

The right-hand triads and suspensions are using some 16th-note syncopations (in particular, landing on the second 16th of beat 4), in conversation with the left-hand thumb playing rhythmic pickups. All this is typical of the funkier contemporary rock piano styles.

Our last voicing example is in the key of F minor, and uses diatonic triads and dyads (two-note intervals).

Modern Rock Voicing Example #3

🔊 Track 63

On beat 1 of each measure we see diatonic triads in F minor, with inversions to voice lead suitably from one measure to the next. Then on beat 3 of each measure, the outer two notes of each inverted triad are played, followed by the inner note on beat 4.

The two-note intervals on beat 3 of each measure can also be referred to as dyads; they create a light, open texture suitable for modern styles. This is all supported with root notes played in octaves, in the left hand.

Next, we'll apply these triads and intervals, in a mellow 16th-note rock comping pattern.

Modern Rock Style Example #3

Track 64

Here, the first four measures are rhythmically sparse, with more subdivisions being added in the last four measures. Again, this simple, open texture is suitable for various modern applications.

CHAPTER 13

MODERN R&B

As mentioned in Chapter 4, the term R&B is a catch-all style category, incorporating soul, funk, hip-hop, dance-pop, and so on. The term Modern R&B is commonly associated with the neo-soul, hip-hop, and R&B/pop recordings from the 2000s onward. These styles sometimes still use the denser voicings we explored for Classic R&B, alongside sparser voicings and more open textures. Both eighth- and 16th-note rhythms are commonly used.

Our first voicing example is in the key of E minor, and creates an open and simple texture with dyads in the right hand.

Modern R&B Voicing Example #1

Track 65

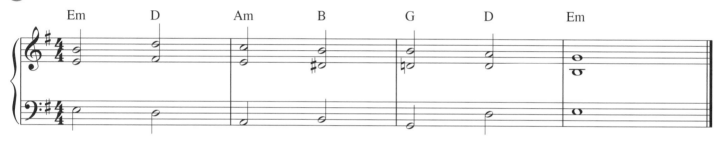

These voicings are based on a triad progression in E minor, using inversions to connect smoothly between chords, but with the middle note of each triad removed.

For example:
Measure 1, Beat 1: The E-B voicing is a root-position E minor triad with the middle note (G) removed.
Measure 1, Beat 3: The F#-D voicing is a 1st-inversion D major triad with the middle note (A) removed.
Measure 2, Beat 1: The E-C voicing is a 2nd-inversion A minor triad with the middle note (A) removed.
Measure 2, Beat 3: The D#-B voicing is a 1st-inversion B major triad with the middle note (F#) removed.
...and so on.
The resulting dyads in the right hand are a useful open texture, as we saw in Chapter 12. Below these simple voicings, the left hand is just playing the root of each chord.
Our first style example uses these voicings in a modern R&B ballad style.

Modern R&B Style Example #1

 Track 66

Note the cut-time meter signature used for this example; this means there are two half-note beats per measure, with the pulse felt on the half-note rather than the quarter note. We could have written this in regular 4/4 time with a 16th-note subdivision (and half the number of measures), but instead we chose cut-time with an eighth-note subdivision.

Why did we do this? Well, in various fakebooks you will see charts of songs that have a 16th-note feel or subdivision, but are notated in cut-time with eighth-notes (and twice the number of measures). Presumably, this is done in an attempt to assist less experienced players. A famous example is the modern R&B song "All of Me" by John Legend, typically notated in cut-time with eighth notes, although it has a straight-16ths rhythmic subdivision and feel.

Track 66 above is notated in this way, to prepare you for this situation when reading a fake book. (If you listen to the backing track, you'll hear the slow 16th-note feel.)

Our next style example uses the same voicings in a more syncopated modern R&B ballad style, this time notated in 4/4 with 16th notes.

Modern R&B Style Example #2

 Track 67

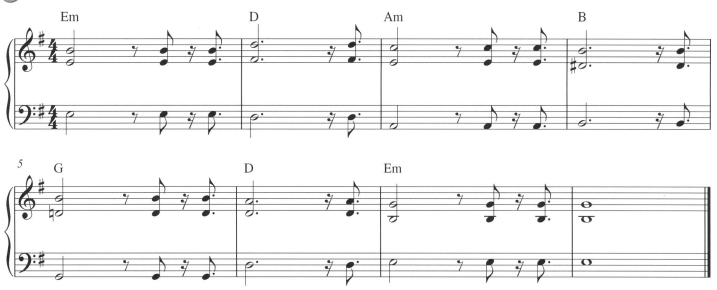

The syncopated effect here is enhanced by the concerted voicings, both hands playing together.

Our next voicing example uses upper-structure block (four-part) chords in the right hand, placed over root notes in the left hand. These voicings are much denser when compared to the previous examples; they are typical of 21st-century neo-soul and more jazz-influenced R&B/pop.

Here we have a mix of voicings for major, minor, and suspended dominant chords, in the key of E minor.

Modern R&B Voicing Example #2

 Track 68

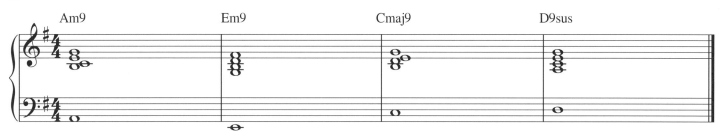

The chord symbols here have been upgraded to five-part (9th) chords to reflect the results of the upper block shapes used. However, as previously noted (see Track 18 and accompanying text), players may apply these voicings to more basic chord symbols if stylistically appropriate. As before, note that the upper-structure block shapes use inversions, to voice lead smoothly through the progression.

Let's take a closer look at the upper-structure block voicings used here:

- In measure 1, the right-hand C major 7th chord is built from the 3rd of the overall Am9 chord.
- In measure 2, the right-hand G major 7th chord is built from the 3rd of the overall Em9 chord.
- In measure 3, the right-hand E minor 7th chord is built from the 3rd of the overall Cmaj9 chord.
- In measure 4, the right-hand A minor 7th chord is built from the 5th of the overall D9sus chord.

Our last style example uses all the right-hand upper-structure block voicings from Track 68, in a modern R&B swing-16ths comping style.

Modern R&B Style Example #3

Track 69

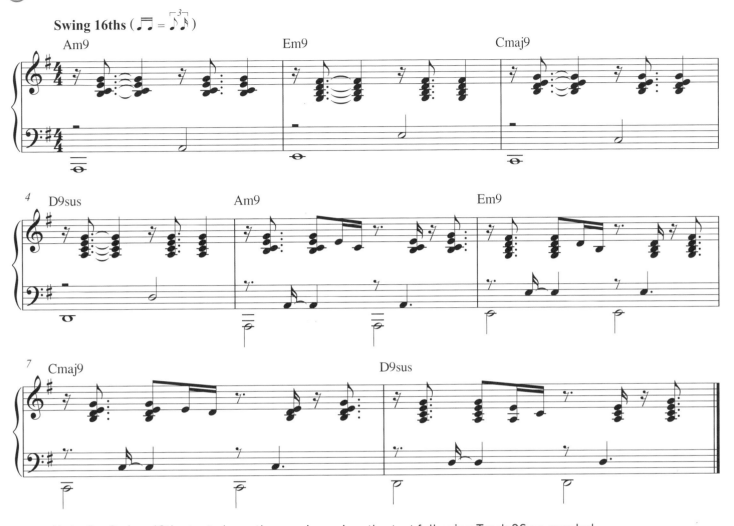

Note the Swing-16ths text above the music; review the text following Track 36 as needed.

In this example, the right-hand voicings are played on the second 16th of beat 1 of each measure, and on backbeats (beat 4 in measures 1-4, and beat 2 in measures 5-8). Meanwhile, the left hand is playing the root of each chord on beats 1 and 3, adding more thumb pickups as the groove progresses.

CHAPTER 14

POP BALLAD

Here, we're using the term Pop Ballad to refer to the slow- to mid-tempo pop styles that use mostly triad harmony and eighth-note rhythms. The heyday for this style was the 1960s to '80s, with some examples occurring in this millennium.

Our first voicing example is in the key of F, and shows a mix of diatonic triads and **bass inversions**.

Pop Ballad Voicing Example #1

Track 70

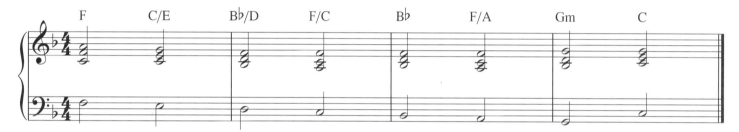

We use the term bass inversion to describe a chord that is inverted over its 3rd or 5th in the bass.

Terminology note: This is not to be confused with upper-triad inversions, which are commonly used to connect between right-hand voicings, as in the above example. Rather, the term bass inversion refers to the placement of the 3rd or 5th of the chord below the triad, in the bass. For example, in the C/E voicing in measure 1 above: we say that the C major triad is "inverted over its 3rd" (E) in the bass, regardless of the actual inversion of the upper C major triad (root position, in this case).

Note that the left-hand line is descending scale-wise within the F major scale: F-E-D-C and so on. For this to occur, and for the harmony to stay diatonic to the key (important for most commercial styles), we are likely to need bass-inversion voicings as described above.

Our first style example uses the voicings from Track 70, in a traditional Pop Ballad style.

Pop Ballad Style Example #1

Track 71

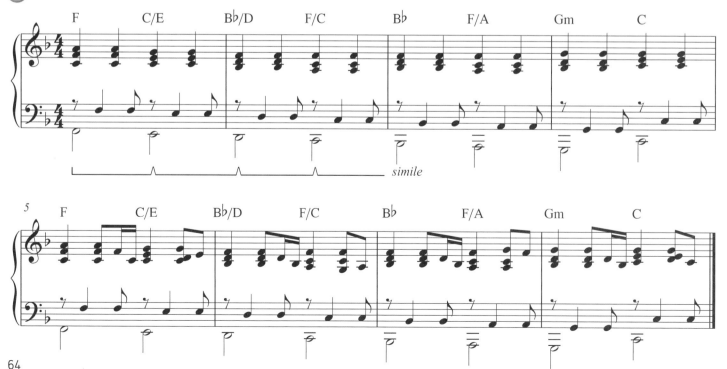

In measures 1-4, the right hand is providing a consistent pulse with quarter-note triads. The left hand is playing the bass notes on beats 1 and 3, and adding the all-important thumb pickups on the upbeats; this provides the eighth-note subdivision needed.

In measures 5-8, the right hand is adding decorative 16th-note subdivisions during beat 2, and interior resolutions within the upper triads during beat 4.

(More about resolutions within triads below).

Our next style example uses the same voicings, with some rhythmic variations.

Pop Ballad Style Example #2
Track 72

On beats 2 and 4 of each measure in this variation, the right hand is playing the outer notes of the triad inversion, followed by single notes in either an eighth- or 16th-note pattern. We saw these dyads before, in Tracks 63-67.

Our next voicing example uses various upper-structure triads and resolutions in the right hand, placed over chord roots in the left hand. As in earlier examples, each individual voicing has a detailed chord symbol for instruction purposes; however, these techniques can be applied to more basic (major or minor) chord symbols as appropriate.

Pop Ballad Voicing Example #2
Track 73

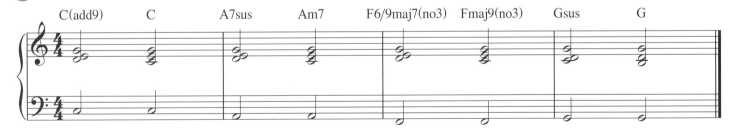

A resolution within a triad normally occurs when we move from the 9th (sometimes called the 2nd) to the root, or from the 4th to the 3rd. These resolutions can occur within a basic triad (i.e., within the triad "built from the root" of the chord symbol), or within an upper-structure triad voicing. Let's see how this works in each measure above, as follows:

Measure 1
- The 9th (D) is moving to the root (C) within the C major triad. This triad is built from the root (C) of the C major chord, creating the Cadd9 to C chord movement.

Measure 2

- The 9th (D) is again moving to the root (C) within the C major triad. This triad is built from the 3rd (C) of the A minor chord, creating the A7sus to Am7 chord movement.

Measure 3

- The 9th (D) is again moving to the root (C) within the C major triad. This triad is built from the 5th (C) of the F major chord, creating the F6/9ma7(no3rd) to Fma9(no3rd) chord movement.

Measure 4

- The 4th (C) is moving to the 3rd (B) within the G major triad. This triad is built from the root (G) of the G major chord, creating the Gsus to G chord movement.

So, on to our last style example, which uses all the upper-structure triads and resolutions from Track 73, in a typical eighth-note Pop Ballad comping style.

Pop Ballad Style Example #3

 Track 74

The right-hand triads and resolutions are all within an octave-doubled hand position; the thumb and pinky should be positioned on the two Gs (above and below middle C) throughout.

In measures 5-8 the rhythmic intensity builds with continuous 8th-note subdivisions in the right hand; the left-hand thumb lands on the backbeats (beats 2 and 4) of each measure.

CHAPTER 15

REGGAE

Reggae is a musical genre that originated in Jamaica in the 1960s. It is noted for its rhythmic syncopations, with staccato chord voicings on upbeats. This style is typically written in 4/4 time with an eighth-note subdivision, but normally has a half-time feel (i.e., the pulse is felt on beats 1 and 3), compared to other contemporary pop styles where the pulse is felt on all the quarter notes (beats 1, 2, 3, and 4).

Our first voicing example is in the key of B minor, and shows a mix of upper-structure triads and four-part voicings.

Reggae Voicing Example #1

Track 75

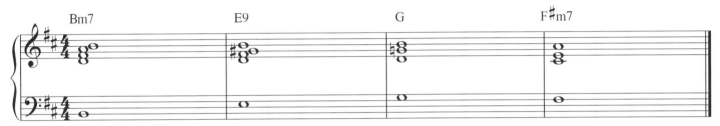

Let's take a look at the right-hand upper-structure triad and block (four-part) voicings used here:
- In measure 1, the right-hand Bm7 block shape is simply built from the root of the overall Bm7 chord.
- In measure 2, the right-hand G#m7(♭5) block shape (in second inversion) is built from the 3rd of the overall E9 dominant chord.
- In measure 3, the right-hand G major triad is simply built from the root of the overall G major chord.
- In measure 4, the right-hand A major triad is built from the 3rd of the overall F#m7 chord.

Note that some of these right-hand voicings are equivalent to the literal spelling of each chord (e.g., for the Bmi7 and G major chords), and some are upper-structure voicings (e.g., for the E9 and F#m7 chords). This type of voicing mix is common across a broad range of contemporary piano styles.

Also in Track 75, the minor 7th and dominant 9th chord symbols reflect the voicings being applied; in other situations, however, we might apply these voicings to more basic chord symbols, depending on the style and context.

Our first style example uses the upper-structure voicings from Track 75.

Reggae Style Example #1

Track 76

Don't forget the Swing-8ths feel when you play this example; it is used for most reggae styles.

In this example, in the odd-numbered measures the right hand is playing a steady quarter-note rhythm on beats 1, 2, and 3, with more eighth-note subdivisions in the even-numbered measures. The left hand is mostly playing the root notes on beat 1, adding pickups and anticipations. Listen to the rhythm track to get comfortable with this half-time reggae feel.

Our next style example uses the same voicings, this time with the right-hand rhythm more centered around beats 2 and 4 in each measure.

Reggae Style Example #2

Track 77

In this example, the right hand begins alone in measures 1-4, for a sparser effect. Then the left hand joins in measures 5-8, with root notes (on beat 1 of each measure) and thumb pickups. Note the syncopation created by the right-hand voicings on the last eighth-note in each measure.

Our next voicing example again uses a mix of upper-structure triads and four-part voicings, all in 2nd inversion.

Reggae Voicing Example #2
Track 78

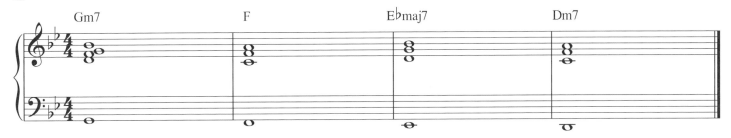

We can analyze these right-hand upper-structure triad and block voicings as follows:

- In measure 1, the right-hand Gm7 block shape is simply built from the root of the overall Gm7 chord.
- In measure 2, the right-hand F major triad is simply built from the root of the overall F major chord.
- In measure 3, the right-hand G minor triad is built from the 3rd of the overall E♭maj7 chord.
- In measure 4, the right-hand F major triad is built from the 3rd of the overall Dm7 chord.

On to our last style example, which uses all the right-hand voicings from Track 78, combined with pentatonic scale riffs in the left hand.

Reggae Style Example #3
Track 79

Note the right-hand emphasis on beats 2 and 4 which, within an overall half-time rhythm section feel, is typical of reggae styles. The left-hand line is based around the roots of each chord, with other connecting tones from the G minor pentatonic scale. (See Chapter 7 text.)

CHAPTER 16

ROCK & ROLL

Rock & Roll is an American music genre that originated in the 1950s from a fusion of the gospel, country, and blues/R&B styles prevalent at the time. This style is noted for its driving rhythms (with mostly eighth-note subdivisions) and energetic piano parts.

Our first voicing example is in C major, and uses the I, IV, and V (one, four, and five) chords typical of the genre. Here, the right-hand voicing consists only of the tonic (C) and the fifth (G) of the key throughout, played over the left-hand voicings for each chord (C, F, and G major, respectively). This technique can be referred to as **voicing over the changes**, as the voicing is chosen with respect to the key of the progression (C major in this case), rather than on a chord-by-chord basis as we have seen for most previous examples.

Rock & Roll Voicing Example #1
Track 80

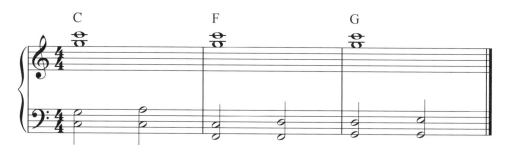

Some vertical tensions against the chords can be created when we voice over the changes in this way; these tensions are typical of Rock & Roll—as well as Blues—styles.

Note that the left-hand voicings are using both root-5th and root-6th intervals for each chord. Alternating between these left-hand intervals during each chord is a staple Rock & Roll sound, as we will see.

Next, let's combine these right-hand 4th intervals and left-hand 5th and 6th intervals to create a driving eighth-note Rock & Roll comping pattern.

Rock & Roll Style Example #1

 Track 81

In the first eight measures, the right hand is simply repeating the G-C 4th interval voicing over each chord, in a steady eighth-note pattern. This is varied in the last eight measures with an F♯ to G half-step movement, below the C top note. The note F♯ here technically comes from the **C Blues scale**: C-E♭-F-F♯-G-B♭. The blues scale is commonly used in Blues and Rock & Roll styles.

In contemporary keyboard styles, a repeated top note in the right hand can be referred to as a drone note. Therefore, we could say that a drone note of C is played in the right hand throughout Track 81.

Meanwhile, the left hand is alternating between root-5th and root-6th interval voicings for each chord, in a steady quarter-note pattern. All this is typical of Rock & Roll piano styles.

Our next voicing example is in the key of G, this time using dominant 7th chords built from the tonic, 4th, and 5th degrees of the key. Dominant 7th chords are often built from the I, IV and/or V chord in this way, in Blues-related styles such as Gospel and Rock & Roll. (Check out our earlier chapters on Blues and Gospel styles for more examples of this.)

The next example also uses Mixolydian 3rd intervals, above a repeated root of the chord, in the right hand. This is similar to the 2nd-inversion Mixolydian triads used in Track 37, except we're selecting two-note 3rd intervals (rather than three-note triads) from the Mixolydian mode corresponding to each dominant chord, respectively. (Review Chapter 8 text accompanying Track 37, as needed.)

Rock & Roll Voicing Example #2

Track 82

We can analyze these right-hand voicings, and compare them to Track 37, as follows:

- In the first measure, we see the following 3rd intervals on top: B-D, C-E, D-F, and back to C-E. These are all from the G Mixolydian mode, and collectively work to define a big-tent G7 dominant chord. Each voicing is also the top two notes of a corresponding triad in the first measure of Track 37: B diminished, C major, or D minor. Below these intervals in Track 82, the thumb is repeating the root of the chord (G).

- In the second measure, we see the following 3rd intervals on top: E-G, F-A, G-B♭, and back to F-A. These are all from the C Mixolydian mode, and collectively work to define a big-tent C7 dominant chord. Each voicing is also the top two notes of a corresponding triad in the second measure of Track 37: E diminished, F major, or G minor. Below these intervals in Track 82, the thumb is repeating the root of the chord (C).

- In the third measure, we see the following 3rd intervals on top: F#-A, G-B, A-C, and back to G-B. These are all from the D Mixolydian mode, and collectively work to define a big-tent D7 dominant chord. Each voicing is also the top two notes of a corresponding triad in the third measure of Track 37: F# diminished, G major, or A minor. Below these intervals in Track 82, the thumb is repeating the root of the chord (D).

Meanwhile, the left-hand voicings are a mix of root-5th and root-6th (13th) intervals, to complement and reinforce the right-hand voicings.

Our next style example takes the three-note right-hand voicings from Track 82 and splits them by playing the top two notes (the Mixolydian 3rd interval) on all the downbeats (beats 1, 2, 3, and 4), and the bottom note (the root of each chord) on the upbeats in between. This creates a typical Rock & Roll and Blues-Rock comping pattern.

Rock & Roll Style Example #2

 Track 83

Note the Swing-8ths text above the music; listen to the audio track to check out the Rock & Roll shuffle feel.

In the last four measures in the right hand, some half-step grace notes have been added. These approach either the 3rd or the 5th of the chord by half-step, a common procedure in Rock & Roll and other Blues-related styles.

Our last voicing example is a variation on Track 82. We are still using Mixolydian 3rd intervals, but now with more voice leading (closer connection) between chords.

Rock & Roll Voicing Example #3

 Track 84

Comparing this example to Track 82, we see that measure 1 is the same. The left-hand voicings are the same in measures 2-3, although transposed down one octave this time. In the right-hand voicings of measures 2-3, however, we observe the following:

- In the second measure, we now see the following 3rd intervals on top: B♭-D, C-E, D-F, and back to C-E. Again, these are all from the C Mixolydian mode, and collectively help define the C7 chord, but are now in the same register as the last measure, creating closer voice leading. Below these intervals, the thumb is now playing the 5th of the chord (G).

- In the third measure, we now see the following 3rd intervals on top: C-E, D-F♯, E-G, and back to D-F♯. Again, these are all from the D Mixolydian mode, and collectively help define the D7 chord, but are now in the same register as the last two measures, to continue the previous voice leading. Below these intervals, the thumb is now playing the 5th of the chord (A).

- Our last style example is a variation on Track 83, with the new right-hand voicings from Track 84.

Rock & Roll Style Example #3

Track 85

As before, half-step grace notes have been added in the last four measures in the right hand. This time, though, on the C7 and D7 chords, the note being targeted is either the 7th or the 9th of the chord, rather than the 3rd or 5th. This is a nice way to spice up your Rock & Roll, and Blues-related piano styles!

CHAPTER 17

SINGER-SONGWRITER

Singer-Songwriter is a rather broad musical category that can encompass anyone who sings and performs their own material. However, the term typically refers to acoustic pop styles with solo vocals, which can be accompanied by a single instrument such as piano or guitar. This genre originated in the 1960s and continues to the present day.

Our first voicing example is in the key of A minor, and mostly uses upper-block (four-part) voicings in the right hand, over root notes in the left hand.

Singer-Songwriter Voicing Example #1

Track 86

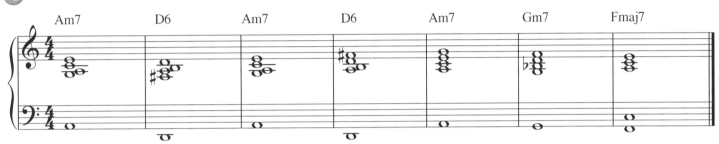

Note that the upper-structure block shapes use inversions, to voice lead smoothly through the progression. Let's take a closer look at the upper-structure block voicings used here:

- In measures 1 and 3, the right-hand C major 7th (in 3rd inversion) is built from the 3rd of the overall Am7 chord, upgrading it to an Am9 in total.
- In measures 2 and 4, the right hand D6 (in 1st and 2nd inversions, respectively) is simply built from the root of the overall D6 chord; note that this is also an inversion of a Bm7 chord.
- In measure 5, the right-hand Am7 is simply built from the root of the overall Am7 chord.
- In measure 6, the right-hand Gm7 is simply built from the root of the overall Gm7 chord.
- In measure 7, the right-hand A minor triad is built from the 3rd of the overall Fmaj7 chord.

Note the mix of right-hand voicing techniques used here:

- Some of these voicings are equivalent to the literal spelling of the chord symbol (e.g., for the D6 and Gm7 chords, and the last Am7 chord).
- Some of these voicings are upper-structure voicings that don't upgrade the chord symbol (e.g., for the Fmaj7 chord).
- Some of these voicings are upper-structure voicings that do upgrade the chord symbol (e.g., for the first two Am7 chords).

Again, this type of voicing mix is common across many contemporary piano styles. Let your ears be the judge!

Our first style example uses the upper-structure voicings from Track 86, together with some left-hand pentatonic scale connecting lines.

Singer-Songwriter Style Example #1

🔊 Track 87

This example uses mostly concerted eighth-note rhythms between the hands, with a few left-hand connecting tones from the D and F pentatonic scales.

Our next voicing example is in G major, and is based on open triad arpeggios in the left hand, together with diatonic 6th intervals in the right hand. (We saw these techniques in Tracks 8 and 9; review as needed.) These are important tools for the Singer-Songwriter pianist.

> Quick reminder
> **Open triad** refers to a triad with its middle note moved up by one octave.
> **Diatonic 6th** refers to 6th intervals which belong to the key of the song.

Singer-Songwriter Voicing Example #2

🔊 Track 88

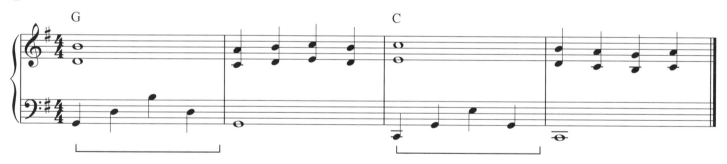

We can analyze the above example as follows:

Right Hand

- On beat 1 of measures 1 and 3, the points of chord change, the 6th intervals are incomplete G major and C major triads, respectively. We saw this type of dyad voicing in earlier examples.

- In measures 2 and 4, the 6th intervals are derived from adjacent scale tones to the above. Note how they lead melodically into the points of chord change.

Left Hand

- For each chord, the left hand is playing an open triad (root-5th-3rd) pattern. See Track 8 and accompanying text.

Our last style example uses the right-hand 6th intervals and left-hand patterns from Track 88, in a classic 16th-note singer-songwriter comping pattern.

Singer-Songwriter Style Example #2

Track 89

The 16th-note subdivisions gently propel the groove, without the more accented syncopations one might hear in some of the R&B and Funk styles.

CHAPTER 18

SMOOTH JAZZ

Smooth Jazz is a sub-style of Contemporary Jazz, which emerged in the 1980s following the birth of Jazz-Rock Fusion in the 1960s. Smooth Jazz emphasizes accessible melodies and commercial production, most often within a light R&B or Funk rhythmic framework.

Our first voicing example uses upper-structure triads in the right hand, over a mix of root-5th and root-7th intervals in the left hand.

Smooth Jazz Voicing Example #1

 Track 90

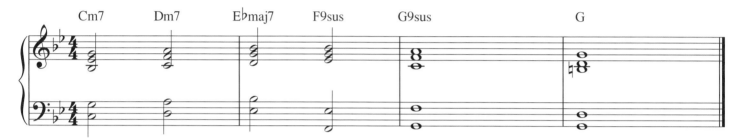

Let's take a look at the upper-structure triad voicings used here:
- In measure 1 (beat 1), the right-hand E♭ major triad is built from the 3rd of the overall Cm7 chord.
- In measure 1 (beat 3), the right-hand F major triad is built from the 3rd of the overall Dm7 chord.
- In measure 2 (beat 1), the right-hand G minor triad is built from the 3rd of the overall E♭maj7 chord.
- In measure 2 (beat 3), the right-hand E♭ major triad is built from the 7th of the overall F9sus chord.
- In measure 3, the right-hand F major triad is built from the 7th of the overall G9sus chord.
- In measure 4, the right-hand G major triad is simply built from the root of the G major chord.

In this style, the left-hand root-5th voicings are common for the major and minor chords, with the root-7th voicings helping to define the suspended dominant chords. As noted earlier, ensure that root-7th intervals are not played too low on the keyboard.

In this case, the voicings are adding no extra chord tones/extensions with respect to the chord symbols used. As seen before, however, these techniques might be used in response to more basic symbols, if desired.

Our first style example uses the upper-structure triad voicings from Track 90, in an up-tempo Smooth Jazz comping style.

Here we build the rhythmic intensity gradually during the 16 measures (four repeats of the original four-measure phrase in Track 90).

- In measures 1-4, we play the basic voicings in a concerted (hands together) style, with some eighth-note anticipations.
- In measures 5-8, we start to arpeggiate (play the voicings in a broken-chord style) in the right hand.
- In measures 9-16, the right hand builds further with octave-doubled triads (triads with a doubled octave on the top and bottom); the hand position is similar to Track 74.

Our next voicing example uses upper-structure double-4th shapes in the right hand, placed over root notes in the left hand. We've used double-4th shapes in various earlier styles. (See the introduction to Chapter 5.) Quick reminder: double-4th is a term we use to describe a three-note shape consisting of one perfect 4th interval above another.

In Jazz, Funk, and Fusion styles, these shapes can be built from the 4th and 5th of a minor or minor 7th chord.

Smooth Jazz Voicing Example #2

Track 92

In measures 1-2, we've built double-4th shapes from the 4th (11th) and 5th of each minor 7th chord in the right hand, as follows:

- In measure 1, the F-B♭-E♭ and G-C-F double-4ths are built from the 4th (F) and 5th (G) of the Cm7 chord, respectively.

- In measure 2, the A♭-D♭-G♭ and B♭-E♭-A♭ double-4ths are built from the 4th (A♭) and 5th (B♭) of the E♭m7 chord, respectively.

In measure 3, we see a four-part block upper-structure: an Fm7 built from the 5th of the B♭9sus (suspended dominant) chord. See Track 18 (measure 7).

Our final style example uses all the right-hand upper-structure double-4th and block voicings from Track 92, in a swing-16ths smooth jazz style.

Smooth Jazz Style Example #2

Track 93

Note the Swing-16ths text above the music; review Track 36 and accompanying text as needed. Enjoy!

FURTHER READING INDEX

Many of the audio tracks in this book, use harmony and voicing techniques that are explained in more detail in my other Hal Leonard publications.

For your convenience, here is a brief index of piano voicing and harmony techniques, showing the tracks in this book that use the technique, and the appropriate references to my other books.

At the end is a list showing the full titles and product numbers for all the books included in the index.

Alternating-triad comping
Audio Tracks 14, 15, 39, 40

The Pop Piano Book (Chapter 12)
Rock Piano Chops (Chapter 2)

Backcycled (IV-I) triads
Audio Tracks 39, 40

The Pop Piano Book (Chapters 17-18)
Blues Piano (Chapter 4)

Bass-inversion voicings
Audio Tracks 70, 71

Pop Piano Book (Chapter 11)
How To Harmonize On The Piano (Chapter 3)

Blues progressions
Audio Tracks 2, 3, 5

Jazz-Blues Piano book (Chapter 4)

Blues piano styles
Audio Tracks 2, 3, 5, 81, 83, 85

Blues Piano book (Chapters 3-6)

Blues scales
Audio Track 81

Blues Piano (Chapter 5)
Contemporary Music Theory Level Two (Chapter 9)

Calm Piano styles
Audio Tracks 6, 7, 8, 9, 10

Piano Zen (Chapters 2-7)

Circle-of-5ths and circle-of-4ths
Audio Tracks 11, 12

All About Music Theory (Chapter 3)
Contemporary Music Theory Level One (Chapter 1)

Country piano styles
Audio Tracks 27, 28, 29, 30, 31

The Pop Piano Book (Chapter 16)
Country Piano (Chapters 3-6)

Dominant 7th chords
Audio Tracks 1, 2, 3, 4, 5, 25, 26, 35, 36, 37, 38, 48, 49, 50, 51, 52, 53, 54, 55, 56, 57, 58, 75, 76, 77, 82, 83, 84

Contemporary Music Theory Level One (Chapter 6)
Blues Piano (Chapters 2-6)
Jazz-Blues Piano (Chapters 3-7)

Dominant 7th chord alterations
Audio Tracks 25, 26, 48, 49, 57, 58

Contemporary Music Theory Level Three (Chapters 8-11)
Contemporary Jazz Piano (Chapters 3-6)

Dorian triads
Audio Tracks 23, 24

The Pop Piano Book (Chapter 15)
Jazz-Blues Piano (Chapter 3)
Contemporary Jazz Piano (Chapter 3)

Dyads (incomplete triads)
Audio Tracks 63, 64, 65, 66, 72, 88, 89

Modern Pop Keyboard (Chapter 3)

Filled-in octave right-hand voicing
Audio Tracks 55, 56, 59, 60

The Pop Piano Book (Chapter 11)
Rock Piano Chops (Chapter 1)

Funk piano styles
Audio Tracks 33, 34, 36, 49, 69, 93

The Pop Piano Book (Chapter 15)
R&B Keyboard (Chapters 4-5)
Jazz-Rock Piano Chops (Chapters 1-4)

Gospel piano styles
Audio Tracks 37, 38, 39, 40, 41

The Pop Piano Book (Chapters 17-18)

Jazz-Fusion piano styles
Audio Tracks 48, 49, 50, 51, 52

Contemporary Jazz Piano (Chapters 3-6)
Jazz-Rock Piano Chops (Chapters 1-4)
Jazz-Blues Piano (Chapter 5)

Jazz Swing piano styles
Audio Tracks 53, 54, 55, 56, 57, 58

Intro To Jazz Piano (Chapters 2-6)
Jazz-Blues Piano (Chapters 3-7)

Minor pentatonic-4th right-hand intervals
Audio Tracks 32, 33, 34

The Pop Piano Book (Chapter 12)
Rock Piano Chops (Chapter 2)

Mixolydian-3rd intervals
Audio Tracks 82, 83, 84

Blues Piano (Chapter 4)
Piano Fitness (Chapter 2)

Mixolydian triads
Audio Tracks 37, 38, 50, 51, 52

The Pop Piano Book (Chapters 15, 17, 18)
Blues Piano (Chapters 4, 6)
Jazz-Blues Piano (Chapters 3, 5, 7)

Modes/modal scales
Audio tracks 23, 24, 37, 38, 50, 51, 52

Contemporary Music Theory Level One (Chapter 5)
How To Harmonize On The Piano (Chapter 4)

Open-triad left-hand arpeggios
Audio tracks 8, 9, 10, 88, 89

The Pop Piano Book (Chapter 11)
Piano Zen (Chapters 3-7)

Pentatonic scales
Audio Tracks 12, 27, 29, 31, 32, 33, 34

Contemporary Music Theory Level Two (Chapter 9)
Piano Fitness (Chapter 2)

Polychord voicings
Audio Tracks 21, 22, 25, 26, 55, 56, 57, 58

Contemporary Jazz Piano (Chapter 3)
Contemporary Music Theory Level Three
  (Chapters 4-12)

Pop Ballad piano styles
Audio Tracks 70, 71, 72, 73, 74

The Pop Piano Book (Chapter 11)

Power-chord (root-5th) voicings
Audio Tracks 11, 13, 59, 60

The Pop Piano Book (Chapter 12)
Rock Piano Chops (Chapters 1-2)
Beginning Rock Keyboard (Chapter 2)

R&B piano styles
Audio Tracks 16, 17, 18, 19, 20, 65, 66, 67, 68, 69

The Pop Piano Book (Chapters 14-15)
R&B Keyboard (Chapter 4)

Resolutions within upper-structure triads
Audio Tracks 61, 62, 73, 74

The Pop Piano Book (Chapters 8-9)

Rock piano styles
Audio Tracks 11, 12, 13, 14, 15, 59, 60, 61, 62, 63, 64

The Pop Piano Book (Chapter 12)
Rock Piano Chops (Chapters 2-4)
Modern Pop Keyboard (Chapters 4-5)

Rock & Roll piano styles
Audio Tracks 80, 81, 82, 83, 84, 85

Blues Piano (Chapters 5-6)

Root-7th left-hand voicings
Audio Tracks 16, 17, 18, 19, 48, 49, 53, 54, 90, 91

Intro To Jazz Piano (Chapters 2-6)
Jazz-Blues Piano (Chapters 3-7)

Seven-three voicings
Audio Tracks 1, 2, 3, 35, 36

Intro To Jazz Piano (Chapters 2-6)
Jazz-Blues Piano (Chapters 3-7)

Seven-three extended voicings
Audio Tracks 1, 3, 25, 26, 57, 58

Intro To Jazz Piano (Chapters 3-6)
Jazz-Blues Piano (Chapters 3-7)

Shape Concept for chord voicings
Used throughout, but in particular:
Audio Tracks 21, 22, 25, 26, 55, 56, 57, 58

Contemporary Music Theory Level Three
  (Chapters 3-12)

Sixth intervals below right-hand melody
Audio Tracks 9, 88, 89

The Pop Piano Book (Chapter 11)
Piano Zen (Chapter 6)

Smooth Jazz piano styles
Audio Tracks 90, 91, 92, 93

Smooth Jazz Piano (Chapters 3-6)
Contemporary Jazz Piano (Chapter 4)

Suspended dominant 7th chords
Audio Tracks 18, 19, 20, 35, 36, 68, 69, 90, 91, 92, 93

Contemporary Music Theory Level One (Chapter 9)
Contemporary Music Theory Level Three (Chapter 8)

Swing-8ths rhythms
Audio Tracks 2, 3, 5, 12, 22, 24, 26, 31, 38, 51, 54, 56, 58, 76, 77, 79, 83, 85

Pop Piano Book (Chapter 2)
Rock Piano Chops (Chapter 2)
Jazz-Rock Piano Chops (Chapter 2)

Swing-16ths rhythms
Audio Tracks 36, 52, 62, 69, 93

Pop Piano Book (Chapter 2)
Rock Piano Chops (Chapter 2)
Jazz-Rock Piano Chops (Chapter 2)

Upper-structure double-4th voicings
Audio Tracks 21, 22, 25, 26, 48, 49, 57, 58, 92, 93

Pop Piano Book (Chapter 10)
Piano Fitness (Chapter 5)
Contemporary Music Theory Level Three (Chapter 3)

Upper-structure four-part voicings
Audio Tracks 4, 5, 18, 19, 20, 48, 49, 53, 54, 55, 56, 68, 69, 75, 76, 77, 92, 93

The Pop Piano Book (Chapter 7)
Intro To Jazz Piano (Chapters 2-3)
Contemporary Music Theory Level Two (Chapter 8)

Upper-structure triad voicings
Audio Tracks 14, 15, 16, 17, 48, 49, 57, 58, 73, 74, 75, 76, 77, 78, 79, 86, 87, 90, 91

The Pop Piano Book (Chapter 5)
Contemporary Music Theory Level Two (Chapter 7)

Walkups and walkdowns
Audio Tracks 30, 31

The Pop Piano Book (Chapters 16 and 18)
Country Piano (Chapter 3)

Here are the full titles and Hal Leonard product numbers for all of the above books:

Book Title	Product No.
All About Music Theory	HL00311468
Blues Piano: The Complete Guide With Audio	HL00311007
Contemporary Jazz Piano: The Complete Guide With Audio	HL00311848
Contemporary Music Theory, Level One	HL00220014
Contemporary Music Theory, Level Two	HL00220015
Contemporary Music Theory, Level Three	HL00290538
Country Piano: The Complete Guide With Audio	HL00312088
How To Harmonize On The Piano	HL00292957
Intro To Jazz Piano: The Complete Guide With Audio	HL00311848
Jazz-Blues Piano: The Complete Guide With Audio	HL00311243
Jazz-Rock Piano Chops	HL00119628
Modern Pop Keyboard: The Complete Guide With Audio	HL00146596
Piano Fitness	HL00311995
The Pop Piano Book	HL00220011
Piano Zen	HL00350216
R&B Keyboard: The Complete Guide With Audio	HL00310881
Rock Piano Chops	HL00312273
Smooth Jazz Piano: The Complete Guide With Audio	HL00311095